DYNAMITE ON ICE:
The Bobby Orr Story

by HAL BOCK

D0311377

An Associated Features Book

SCHOLASTIC BOOK SERVICES
New York Toronto London Auckland Sydney Tokyo

To Fran and Richard

Copyright © 1972 by Associated Features, Inc. This edition is published by Scholastic Book Services, a division of Scholastic Magazines, Inc., by arrangement with Associated Features, Inc.

1st printing .... February 1972

Printed in the U.S.A.

CONTENTS

Chapter 1

SUDDEN DEATH

BOBBY Orr sat at his locker in the steamy Boston Bruin dressing room, his head bent and the beads of perspiration falling off his forehead.

It was the middle of May — a strange time for a hockey game — and the Bruins were awaiting the start of the overtime period in the fourth game of the 1970 National Hockey League Stanley Cup play-offs.

The Bruins had won the first three games of the final-round series against the St. Louis Blues and needed just one more victory to clinch the cherished Cup. Now, with the game tied at the end of regulation play, it would be "sudden death." The first team to score would win. One goal. That's all it would take.

"I knew I had to do something," said Orr, the marvelous young defenseman who had won the NHL scoring championship with 120 points that season. "I hadn't done a thing in the whole series."

Soon it was time for the Bruins to return to the ice and Orr laced up his skates and trudged through the door over the rubber mat that led from the dressing room to the rink. The score was tied at 3-3 and Orr, the scoring champion, hadn't even achieved an assist. It had been a frustrating game for the 22-year-old star.

"I was thinking about it a lot in the room before the overtime started," said Orr. "An awful lot."

The Bruins had steamed into the championship series by first eliminating New York and then Chicago in the preliminary Stanley Cup rounds. That set up the final series against St. Louis and created an enormous problem for Scotty Bowman, coach of the Blues. The problem: How to stop Bobby Orr?

Orr had scored eight goals in the Bruins' first 10 play-off games against the Rangers and Black Hawks. During the regular season, he had accumulated 33 goals and 87 assists, becoming the first defenseman in history to win the scoring crown.

Orr is the man around whom Boston's awesome attack is built. His electrifying rushes up ice freeze opposing defensemen and, more often than not, they end up with Orr or one of his teammates blasting the puck toward the net.

Controlling him was, of course, Scotty Bowman's Number One headache as St. Louis prepared to face the Bruins.

"I don't think we have a chance at all against Boston unless we can stop Orr," said Bowman. And the inventive St. Louis boss thought he had a way to do that.

"They've always said they're glad Bobby is a defenseman," said Bowman, "because he can't be checked. I say he can be and we will do it. It's our only chance to beat them."

What Bowman did was assign one of his forwards, usually Jimmy Roberts, to follow Orr all over the ice and check him. Shadows have been used to track high scorers before in an attempt to control their output, but never had a team assigned one of its forwards to check an opposing defenseman. The strategy had the immediate disadvantage of breaking up the Blues' attacking pattern because one St. Louis forward was doing nothing but checking Orr.

7

"We are trying to force them to make their plays some place else," Bowman explained. "The plan is to keep the puck away from Orr and to have someone on him all of the time."

The Bruins expected special treatment for Bobby simply because Bobby is a special kind of hockey player. But they never expected the total sacrifice of one attacker to check one of their defensemen.

Early in the first game of the play-offs, Roberts, the Number One shadow, said to Orr, "I guess we're giving you the Bobby Hull treatment, eh." Orr, slightly dismayed by the whole thing, simply grunted.

"I was surprised at the shadow," Orr said later. "I expected to be watched, but not like that. I might as well have gone out to lunch for all I had to do with the game. I just tried to stay out of the way."

His shadow notwithstanding, Orr did manage one assist in Boston's 6-1 first-game victory. The success of the Bruins in scoring without Orr's help did not alter Bowman's strategy. He stayed with the shadow idea.

"I thought it was effective on Orr," said Bowman. "There are two advantages to the strategy. He starts a lot of plays so at least they'll have to pass some place else, and he's always in front of their net and that's a good place for one of our guys to be too."

8

Roberts, an excellent defensive player, seemed the logical choice as Orr's shadow. "He scored 120 points," said Roberts. "You've got to come up with something. Maybe this is a start. It's our best idea so far. The strategy is for me to worry about where he might go or what he might do. It's just so the others won't pass him the puck."

That's just what happened in the opener. The Bruins started going elsewhere with the puck, with no significant limitation on their attack's efficiency. The hole in Bowman's strategy was that, by using one of his forwards to check and follow only Orr, he was leaving a gap in his defense. But the Blues figured it was worth the investment if it helped them control Bobby.

"He's the one who starts it all. We can sacrifice one of our guys if that's what it takes to cover him," said Roberts. "He's more valuable than any one of us." Or any two or three, he might have added. It's a cinch that Bowman, the Blues' general manager, could have offered half a dozen of his athletes in exchange and not been able to get Orr away from the Bruins.

Bowman stayed with the shadow strategy in the second and third games of the series. In Game Two, Orr managed two assists, but he was shut out in Game Three.

DICK RAPHAEL

Despite close checking by the Blues, Bobby Orr got off several hard shots like this one in St. Louis.

However, although they had Orr under reasonable control, the Blues had been unable to cope with the rest of the Bruins, and so in Game Four, Bowman decided to have his club return to conventional hockey. There was no shadow for Orr and the change in approach very nearly paid off for the Blues.

The fourth game of the series marked the only time the Blues ever led the Bruins. In fact, with just over six minutes remaining, St. Louis was still in front. But then the Bruins tied it, forcing the sudden-death overtime. Orr, left to his own devices, had not dominated play offensively as he had so often during the regular season.

In the dressing room as the Bruins prepared for the extra period, coach Harry Sinden said little. What could he say to a team playing its 100th hockey game of the season in the middle of May?

Sinden decided to start the overtime period with a rush. "Let's play offensive hockey," he told his skaters. "Go after them. Pin them in their own end."

The words were ringing in Orr's ears as he stepped onto the ice. "Get the puck in their end and keep it there," he thought as the two teams prepared for the face-off. Sinden assigned Orr and Don Awrey on defense with Derek Sanderson's line up front for the start of the overtime.

Most of the fans in ancient Boston Garden were on their feet as the puck was dropped, starting the extra period. But there was one empty spot in the stands. Doug Orr, a visitor from Parry Sound, Ontario, whose son plays defense for the Bruins, had left his seat.

"When the game was tied," Doug Orr recalled afterward, "I went out underneath the stands. I was walking back and forth under there."

The senior Orr was still pacing when the overtime started. The Bruins won the opening face-off and the puck shot into the St. Louis zone — just where Coach Sinden wanted it. As the disc came out from behind the Blues' net, it skipped past a couple of Boston players and Bobby Orr skated in from the blue line to try and help out.

"I remember," said Don Awrey, Orr's defense partner, "thinking to myself that if Bobby missed the puck, they'll break out three-on-one, and that I'll be the one."

Orr did not miss. He blocked the puck and got it to Sanderson, who was now stationed behind the net. The Blues shifted their attention to Sanderson, who waited just long enough to make sure that St. Louis had forgotten about Orr, the man they had watched so intently for the first three games of the series. Even goalie Glenn Hall turned to see what Sanderson was doing back there.

Finally, at precisely the right moment, Sanderson flipped the puck back in front. Orr zoomed in on it like a hungry bird swooping down on a bread crumb. Orr's stick met the puck directly in front of goalie Hall and banged the frozen rubber into the net.

Just then, Noel Picard, a robust St. Louis defenseman, arrived on the scene and pitchforked Orr up into the air. As the Boston fans exploded in excitement at the red light that signaled the Stanley Cup winning goal, Bobby Orr seemed to float serenely to the ice, making a soft landing to the right of the St. Louis net.

The frenzy that tore through Boston Garden was to be expected. The Bruins had last won a Stanley Cup in 1941 — seven years before Bobby Orr was born. It had been a long, long wait.

And underneath the stands, Doug Orr, the visitor from Parry Sound, peeked out to see what all the yelling was about.

UPI

It's a goal! Bobby Orr scores and the Bruins win their first Stanley Cup in 29 years.

Chapter 2

PARRY SOUND

PARRY Sound is a peaceful, pleasant town on the lip of the Georgian Bay in the northern reaches of Canada's vast Ontario province. It's 150 miles away from the hustle and bustle of Toronto and light years removed in its serenity.

The population is about 6,000 and most of the people know one another. It is a warm, closely-knit community, proud of its clean streets, fresh air, and junior hockey program.

The profile of the town is dominated by the huge Canadian National Railways trestle. The trestle is a reminder of Parry Sound's railroading heritage. The town was established in Canada's pioneer days as a lumbering camp, and in order to service the mills, the Canadian National Railways and Canadian Pacific Railroads both extended their tracks into map-dot Parry Sound.

The trestle, straddling the Seguin River, stands as a tribute to the hardy breed of citizens who first settled there. As the town grew, it attracted new inhabitants, one of them a professional soccer player from Ireland named Robert Orr.

Robert Orr moved to Parry Sound in the early 1900's and raised his family there. One of his sons, Doug, was an unusually gifted young athlete. In fact, in 1939 Doug Orr was voted the Number One performer at the Parry Sound High School Track Meet.

There are some who say that Doug Orr was such a good hockey player that he could have made it to the National Hockey League. It is something he wonders about sometimes; he'll never know. He had a chance for a tryout after his high school days but his adventurous spirit led him to join the Navy instead.

After World War II, Doug Orr and his bride, the former Arva Steele, settled down in Parry Sound. It wasn't long before the house at 24 Great North Road had additional occupants. First there was a girl, Pat, then a boy, Ron.

On March 20, 1948, Arva Orr gave birth to the third of her five children and the Orrs named this one after his grandfather, Robert.

Bobby Orr's arrival into the world at St. Joseph's General Hospital, where his grandmother worked as a nurse, was not at all in keeping with the general serenity of Parry Sound. There were fears for the infant's survival and he had the nurses and doctors scurrying before he pulled through.

Doug Orr was devoted to his children. He spent every spare moment romping with them when not at work at Canadian Industries, an explosives company. Like all Canadian boys, Bobby Orr got his first pair of skates early — at the age of four.

"He was like most kids that age," said Doug Orr. "He'd take a couple of steps, then be over on his ankles. He'd take a stride, flop, bounce right up, and then do it all over again. The hockey stick was mostly for balance."

"I don't really remember it," said Bobby. "But mainly, I imagine I was like any young boy the first time on skates — I couldn't stand up."

It took awhile for young Bob to get his

skating legs, but there were few places better
equipped for him to do it. Parry Sound, with
its subfreezing temperatures, is a winter
wonderland that serves as a perfect setting
for the development of hockey players. The
Seguin River freezes over early and stays
that way for most of the winter, and every
day the ice swarms with hockey-playing
youngsters.

The game at that level is called "shinny"
and the only rules are to keep the puck on
your stick as long as you can. It is considered
the best way to develop the ability to stickhandle, and shinny was Bobby Orr's game.

"We lived down near the Seguin and every
winter we'd build a rink on the river for
the kids," said Doug Orr. "Bob was always
out there, playing shinny with the other
boys."

Young Orr wasn't very big, so he didn't
have to endure too much rough stuff from
the other Parry Sound kids. But he could
certainly handle a puck, and size had nothing
to do with that.

"He could skate right through a whole
team," said Doug. "The other boys wouldn't
try to tackle him too hard because of his
size. I can remember his mother coming
down to the river bank and watching him
go."

His father set up a piece of tin in the Orr garage for young Bobby to shoot at and the puck would smash into the metal for hours on end, often into mealtime. Sometimes Arva Orr would call Bob two and three times before she'd get him in for dinner.

"He could spend hours at a time, just shooting over and over at that single piece of tin," said his dad.

And whatever time young Bob had left over would be spent down on the Seguin, mastering his skating and stickhandling with the rest of the Parry Sound boys.

"I was very lucky," said Bobby. "There was always plenty of ice around. You could skate all of the time if you wanted to."

And Bobby Orr wanted to. Like most Canadian youngsters, he had the National Hockey League on his mind almost as soon as he could take more than one or two strides on the ice without flopping.

Hockey wasn't the only diversion available to a youngster growing up in Parry Sound. There were hunting and fishing trips with his dad, parks and theaters to go to, and the usual activities that keep a boy occupied. But hockey was always Number One with Bobby Orr.

"As his skating developed, so did his stickhandling," said Doug. "You could see it happening slowly but surely."

The more Bobby skated, the less he fell down and soon he didn't fall at all. His ankles, instead of flopping over, would stay ram-rod straight as he dug his blades into the ice and moved gracefully over the frozen surface. His feet would be numb from the frigid temperatures, but the accomplishment of staying up and not resurfacing the ice with his back eased the discomfort of the cold. Bobby Orr was starting to master this game, and he knew it. So did some other people.

After a couple of years on the Seguin, with its makeshift rink, young Bobby was invited indoors. Like most Canadian communities, Parry Sound has its own junior hockey program. Alex Eagar, proprietor of the Brunswick Hilton Hotel, was the moving force behind the Parry Sound Minor Hockey Association. And at just about the time young Orr was ready to start playing in the league, things weren't going terribly well for it.

"I suggested that we had to put a lot of hard work and some money into the program," said Eagar, "and that we'd need a really big man . . . a big name . . . to handle the team."

Eagar and his colleagues in the Parry

Sound hockey group outdid themselves obtaining that big name. They got Bucko Mac-Donald, a former block-busting defenseman for the Toronto Maple Leafs and ex-member of Canada's parliament, to take over the program.

The Community Center where the Parry Sound teams played was a large, cold, unheated structure with seats for about 1,200 spectators. Organized hockey was available for youngsters from kindergarten age up through squirt, pee wee, bantam, midget, and intermediate. And there were more than enough boys to play at every level.

When Orr began playing in the organized league, with stands and a regulation rink, with real nets in place of the makeshift substitutes he'd been brought up with, he was excited. It was much like an American youngster, who has played his baseball on sandlots with his friends, suddenly having his team sponsored and outfitted with uniforms and other accessories. The Parry Sound Community Center might just as well have been Toronto's Maple Leaf Gardens as far as young Bobby Orr was concerned.

"We had always skated outdoors," said Bobby, "so when we started going into the community center, it was a great thrill. My family and friends would come to all the games and they could really shake that old building when they started hollering."

The Community Center was a constant starting point for winter activity in Parry Sound. Almost at any time of the day or night, one could find a hockey game going on. And if you were really lucky, Bobby Orr would be playing when you got there.

Young Bobby turned his share of heads playing for the Parry Sound Pee Wees. "He really started to show good hockey sense when he was about nine years old," said Doug Orr. "He could handle a hockey stick very well for a boy that age."

When Bobby wasn't playing organized hockey in the Community Center, he could be found back out on the river, playing shinny.

"Most of the time, we were on the ice from early morning until darkness," Bobby said. "Sometimes there would be 30 of us, chasing after the same puck. We made up our own games, and we never let the weather bother us."

The temperature sometimes dipped to 40 below zero and the winds whipped across the river at gale force, but still young Orr and his playmates threw the puck around, dipsy-doodling it from one side of the hockey stick to the other, daring the other kids to take it away.

"That's where I learned to stickhandle," said Orr. "If you couldn't grab a puck and keep it, you didn't play much and you didn't have much fun."

But Bobby could keep a puck and did he have fun! As Bobby's stickhandling and other basic hockey talents were honed on the frozen river surface, they began to show up when he played in the Community Center. It wasn't long before Bucko MacDonald's trained eye picked Bobby out from the crowd of Parry Sound youngsters who turned out to learn their hockey from the famous old Toronto star.

"He was really something," said MacDonald. "He could make that puck do tricks on the end of his stick."

Doug Orr, keeping close tabs on his young son, suggested to MacDonald that Bobby might be better off playing forward because of his ability to handle the puck. Doug also figured that a move to forward would improve Bobby's skating too. But MacDonald turned the idea down.

"Anybody can play forward," said Bucko. "Bobby's too smart to waste up there. He belongs on defense. Why, he could be another Doug Harvey some day."

So, the little blond kid with the crew cut stayed on defense. His size made him look out of place, but when he started rushing that puck out of his own end and shrugging off opposing players with head feints and fakes that boys twice his age hadn't mastered, MacDonald knew he had made the right decision.

The Parry Sound Minor Hockey program flourished and soon the town's teams were making short trips to play squads from the other small Ontario communities that dot the Canadian countryside.

"We had a lot of fun," said Orr, "traveling from town to town, playing different teams."

Young Bobby was a leader of the Parry Sound teams, even though he was the smallest boy on the squad. His coaches always knew they could depend on Orr.

Royce Tennet, Bobby's first coach at the Community Center, noticed that the other boys would follow Bob's lead. "He was good with people," said Tennet. "A leader in a quiet sort of way. He was always one of the fun boys on the team."

When Bobby came under Bucko MacDonald's coaching, another aspect of the young man's uniqueness came out. He never had to be told something more than once. It is a quality that made young Orr a dream athlete to coach.

"I had to tell him fewer times than anybody else when there was a mistake to correct," said MacDonald. "One time, we were playing a team from Aurora, Ontario. Bobby made a couple of mistakes and they scored a couple of goals. He came to me and asked me to take him off defense. I said to Bob, 'The only reason that you've asked me to take you off the defense is that you've made two mistakes out there and it cost us a couple of goals. You know, it's kind of nice to see you make mistakes once in awhile. It shows that you're human.' "

A grin wide enough to stretch from one bank of the Seguin River to the other creased young Orr's face.

"Then I said, 'The only reason those mistakes are more noticeable to you is that you don't make them as often as the other boys.' " MacDonald continued. "Then I said, 'Are you ready to go out?' "

Bobby looked up at the crusty old coach and said, "Yes, I am, Bucko, and I'll be playing defense."

"I haven't taken him off there yet," said MacDonald.

Orr's talent for learning fast and applying what he had learned on the ice made him an instant standout for the Parry Sound team. Folks in the friendly little community would jam the Community Center to watch the local boys do their stuff. But the player they watched the most was Bobby Orr.

Bobby was only nine when he won the Most Valuable Pee Wee Award for the province of Ontario, quite an achievement for such a little guy. But on the ice, young Mr. Orr was nine feet tall.

Off the ice, young Bobby was just like the rest of the kids in Parry Sound. He liked to have his fun but was a diligent worker in school, always careful to keep his grades up so that he could continue to play hockey. Winters were for hockey and schoolwork. Summers for swimming, fishing, hunting, and camping with his dad and his brothers.

The Moon River, about 40 miles from Parry Sound, was Bobby's favorite summertime fishing spot. A little luck and a lot of patience could produce an impressive catch of pickerel from the crystal waters of the peaceful river.

"My dad and I always fished the Moon River during the summer," said Bobby. "It's a great spot."

"He was always a good fisherman," said Doug Orr. "He could catch 'em in a bathtub."

Often the Orrs would treat themselves to a shore dinner — after catching the fish and then cooking them. They would feast on their catch at the shore of the river often illuminated by the moon it is named after.

Summers were peaceful for young Bobby, the winters much more hectic. Hockey kept him on the run with the Parry Sound team.

Now it was 1960. Bobby Orr was 12 years old and developing every day into a better hockey player. He and his friends would talk hockey from morning to night, dreaming of the day one of them might play in the National Hockey League.

Meanwhile, in the big league, the Boston Bruins were in the process of finishing fifth among six teams. And the Bruins were dreaming, too, of a young player who might lead them back up the NHL ladder.

Chapter 3

THE SEARCH

THE executive offices of the Boston Bruins are located in Boston Garden, the old building where the team plays its home games. Built as part of the city's North Station complex, the building is a dreary place and that was perfect for the mood of the team's executives as they gathered to consider the Bruins' situation.

Around the league other teams were developing superstars who were dominating play. Montreal had Jean Beliveau ready to follow in the footsteps of the retiring Maurice Richard. Chicago had a young bull named Bobby Hull. Toronto had a flashy left winger, Frank Mahovlich. Detroit had all-time scoring champ Gordie Howe. Even lowly New York had high-scoring Andy Bathgate.

Only the Bruins, it seemed, were left out. The Bruins had no superstar, no outstanding player who could excite the public, no single man who could somehow lift the team out of the doldrums as a Howe could for Detroit or a Beliveau for Montreal. It was a desperate situation and the Boston executives knew it.

President Weston Adams, Sr., summoned a group of Boston club officials to his offices to consider the problem. "What can we do?" Adams asked his staff. The answer, they all agreed, was to search every part of Canada — leaving no rink uncovered — to find the player who could answer Boston's need. Surely in a country as vast as Canada, there had to be an uncommitted player who had the makings of a star. The problem would be to find him.

Wren Blair wasn't at Adams' summit conference. He was busy at the time, running Boston's Kingston, Ontario, franchise in the Eastern Professional League. But Blair had heard about the decision in Boston and suggested to some of his bosses that a good place to start their search might be in Kingston where his team was scheduled to meet a squad from Sault Ste. Marie, Ontario, in a play-off game.

A group of half a dozen Boston officials headed by Adams flew North at Blair's suggestion. But hockey people rarely will go such a distance to see one game. To make the trip worthwhile, Blair arranged for them to take in a bantam provincial play-off game at Gananoque, Ontario, a small town 18 miles east of Kingston.

Usually, hockey talent scouts won't even look at a boy playing at the bantam level simply because he hasn't matured enough to be properly judged. But the quick trip to Gananoque would give the Bostonians a chance to watch another hockey game — and as long as they were so close by, it seemed perfectly reasonable to go.

Besides, Blair had gotten word that there were two defensemen playing that night who would be interesting to watch. One was Rick Eaton and the other was Doug Higgins. Neither was named Bobby Orr.

Young Orr's progress at Parry Sound had been so swift that he had been moved up to play with the bantam group instead of the pee wees. And it just so happened that the team the two promising defensemen from Gananoque were playing on this fateful day was Bobby Orr's Parry Sound club.

As is customary for scouts from an NHL organization to do when they watch prospects, the Boston group split up. Weston Adams sat in one section of the Gananoque rink, Wren Blair went off to another part of the stands; and Lynn Patrick, then Boston's general manager, and Milt Schmidt, the club's coach, sat together in still another section. This allowed the Bruin observers to get different views of the players and the four men agreed to compare notes after the first period.

It didn't take nearly that long for the Bruins' task force to discover Bobby Orr.

"I was sitting there," said Blair, "watching those two defensemen, Eaton and Higgins. And a funny thing kept happening. I saw this little guy on the Parry Sound team out of the corner of my eye. And it seemed I kept going back to him all the time."

It was no different on the other side of the rink where Patrick and Schmidt were seated.

"After two or three minutes of play," said Schmidt, "I turned to Lynn and I said, 'There's a kid on that Parry Sound team . . . either my eyes are going bad on me or something . . . but he looks like something outside of the normal sphere of hockey players at this age. Watch that Parry Sound team for a moment and see if you think it's the same player I do.'

"Lynn looked at me and said, 'You mean that little guy — Number 2?' I said, 'Yeah,' and he said, 'Isn't he something?' "

Young Mr. Orr was something all right. He completely dominated play, carrying the puck out of his own end with the poise of a big leaguer. He made head feints, changes of speed, and moves that completely dazzled the other team, not to mention the Boston people.

Adams, the Bruins' top man, will never forget his first look at young Bobby, who stood all of five-foot-three and weighed perhaps 120 pounds.

"I remember his baggy pants and his shock of blond hair and that he was playing defense although he was one of the smallest boys on the ice," said Blair. "What attracted me most aside from his uniform, the way it fit, was the fact that he was a defenseman. He was a small boy but he was a general. He was directing the team, telling them what to do, doing it himself and seeing to it that they did it too."

Adams knew then that he must have that little guy — that little Number 2 — for the Bruins.

"He had the look of eagles in his eyes," the Bruins' chief said. "He just looked like he was destined for greatness in hockey."

As they had planned to do, the Boston group met after the first period and one couldn't wait to tell the other what he had seen. The simple fact of it was that all of them had seen the same thing. And that was Bobby Orr.

There was no need for any of the Boston executives to sell any of the others on Number 2 for the Parry Sound bantam team. They all agreed that he was something special. What they had to find out was just who this shrimp with the marvelous talent for playing defense was. Blair was sent after the information. He returned quickly with a broad face.

"His name is Bobby Orr," said Blair, "and nobody's sponsoring Parry Sound."

The second fact was every bit as important as the first. If another NHL team had already underwritten the Parry Sound program, young Bobby Orr might not have been available to the Bruins. But the Parry Sound program was independent and that meant that no other team had a claim on Orr.

Bobby Orr was unaware of the excitement he had caused in the stands that day. The only thing on his mind was the score of the game, entirely unsatisfactory from Parry Sound's point of view.

"I remember the game," said Orr. "I know we lost, but I can't say how I played."

Parry Sound had lost the title game in the Ontario bantam play-offs 1-0, but the happiness in the winning dressing room could be matched only by the joy the Boston task force felt over finding this diamond in the rough named Bobby Orr.

Despite the fact that his team lost the championship game, Orr was named the Most Valuable Player in the tournament — an honor he richly deserved, according to Wren Blair.

"He looked like a 12-year-old Doug Harvey," said Blair. "No wasted motions, poise, never got rattled under pressure. He was far and away the best player on the ice."

Bobby Orr, dejected over his team's failure in the provincial play-off, returned to Parry Sound to resume the day-to-day routine of a 12-year-old growing up in this middle-class Ontario community. He was totally unaware of the scheming that was going on in Boston because of his performance in those play-offs.

The Bruins decided that the best route to any Parry Sound hockey player's heart would be straight through the center of the town's junior program. And they were right. So they approached the town with an offer to underwrite the program to the tune of $1,000 per year.

Parry Sound was flabbergasted and delighted, to say the least. Here was an NHL team coming in with a sizable contribution to help their program flourish. The same program that only a few years before — before Bobby Orr, that is — was floundering, now would be financially sound thanks to the Bruins' interest.

Traditionally, Parry Sound had been Toronto country, simply because the Maple Leafs were the closest NHL franchise. There was some support for Montreal too. But Boston? Boston might as well have been Siberia as far as Parry Sound was concerned. That was the sentiment the Bruins had to battle, and their contribution to the hockey program was the first step in breaking down the town's resistance and ultimately the resistance of the little defenseman with the blond crew cut.

The Bruins assigned Blair, a friendly man always quick with a smile, to woo Orr into their organization. If anybody could do it, they figured, Blair was the man. He was a warm, talkative guy who could, if he had to, sell a refrigerator to an Eskimo. And, as things developed, there would be a two-year talkathon with the Orr family.

"He was always around," said Bobby, "talking to mom and dad and me. And every time he took his team north, he stopped off at Parry Sound for a visit."

In the two years Blair spent wooing the Orr family, his assignment in the Boston organization was switched from Kingston to Oshawa, Ontario, where he ran the Bruins' Junior A farm team. Junior A was where the Bruins wanted young Orr.

Blair pleaded his case constantly, and eventually he wore down the resistance of the Orr family. "Let Bobby go to our tryout camp in Niagara Falls," Blair said on one of his visits. "Terry Ainslie is going, so he won't be alone."

Ainslie was one of Orr's hockey-playing buddies from Parry Sound. At least, Bobby's parents reasoned, their boy wouldn't be alone in Niagara Falls.

"Then you'll let him go?" asked Blair.

"O.K.," answered Doug Orr, "he can go."

"You won't be sorry," said Blair. "I can assure you of that."

They shook hands and a few days later Bobby Orr and his friend Terry Ainslie were on the train headed for Niagara Falls and ultimately the National Hockey League.

Chapter 4

OSHAWA

THE little guy with the blond crew cut picked up the puck and took it behind his own net. He waited patiently, while his teammates got into position. Then he started out down the right side of the ice. He shook off the first player who tried to take the puck away, then he did it again to the second one. By now he was at the center red line. Suddenly he picked up speed and zoomed into the attacking zone, carrying the puck easily on the blade of his stick. Like a car shifting speeds, he flashed away from the other players and bore down on the enemy goaltender. He flicked his wrists and the puck flew off his stick into the net.

There was no explosion of applause from the stands, simply because the stands were empty except for a few Boston Bruin scouts and executives. Those were the only people interested enough in the team's annual fall tryout camp to travel to the arena in Niagara Falls, Ontario. The tryout camp, held the week before Labor Day, is a Bruin tradition each year. But this particular camp was especially important to the Boston team. That's because the blond crew cut belonged to a boy named Bobby Orr.

From the moment they first saw Bobby Orr, the Bruins were determined to get the youngster into their organization. The Boston executives watched carefully as young Orr made moves on the ice that left boys three and four years older than he baffled and helpless. He controlled the puck as if he had it attached to a string like a yo-yo.

Weston Adams, president of the Bruins, sat down in the stands next to Wren Blair and said, "We've got to get this boy now."

Blair's assignment was to convince the Orrs to let Bobby join Boston's Junior A farm team at Oshawa, Ontario, and in the process to have him sign an amateur agreement.

Oshawa is a small town some 40 miles east of Toronto and 150 miles south of Parry

Sound. It is a friendly community, but 150 miles might just as well be a million when you're trying to convince a 14-year-old boy's mother that her son should leave home to play ice hockey.

Arva Orr wouldn't hear of it. "He's too young," she argued. "Wait a few years." But Blair had already waited as long as he cared to wait. It had been two years since the Bruins had located young Bobby in that fateful bantam game at Gananoque. "He needs better competition to keep improving," Blair said, trying to persuade Mrs. Orr. "If he stays here, his hockey will suffer."

Doug and Arva Orr and their five children were a close-knit family and Bobby was no more anxious to leave his parents and brothers and sisters than they were to have him go. He enjoyed his family life and the small town of Parry Sound.

"I love Parry Sound," said Bobby. "It's a slow-moving town. Just a small town. Not a lot of traffic. It's a great place to grow up in. Good fishing, good hunting, beautiful parks, good clean water, good clean air. It's just a great place."

But Bobby Orr's talent for hockey would have to be refined elsewhere and Wren Blair was determined that it would be in the Boston Bruins' organization. At that time, young hockey players could be obtained by NHL clubs for future delivery simply by the signing of a form agreement. Blair had one along with him whenever he visited the Orrs, hoping that he'd get that vital dotted line filled with Bobby's signature. Naturally, Blair had the form with him as he headed north for Parry Sound to spend the Labor Day week end of 1962 talking with the Orrs.

"We spent nearly all day Sunday with the family," said Blair. "Mrs. Orr was still hesitant and when you look at it, I guess she had a good point. Here's a boy just 14, being graduated from eighth grade, and talking about leaving home.

"I didn't get him on Sunday. I stayed overnight and went back to the Orrs on Monday. I talked with the father and mother and finally, about noon hour that day, I got Bobby to sign that card."

The Orrs had agreed, but only on certain conditions. First, and most important, Bobby would not be allowed to move to Oshawa. He could play for the Generals, but he would live at home and commute south for the games. That meant a 150-mile ride each way for the youngster, but it was the only way his parents would permit him to sign.

Bobby Orr never really cared what National Hockey League team he would play for in the far-off future. "I played hockey for fun," he said, "and although it was on my mind right from the start that some day I'd like to play in the NHL, I didn't have my heart set on any one team."

By signing Blair's card, Bobby was committing himself to the Bruins.

"My dad and I talked it over," said Bobby. "The Bruins were down on the bottom of the league. I guess I thought they'd be the easiest team to make. They had to go up. Other teams had set line-ups. But Boston. . . . I thought I'd be able to get to the NHL faster with them."

The first stop on the road to Boston would be the Oshawa Generals. Not coincidentally, the major industry in Oshawa is a General Motors factory. The people are fiercely proud of their community and when a fire destroyed the local arena some years before Orr got there, a local drive raised $1.2 million to build a new one. The theme of the building campaign was, "Let's build it by ourselves, for ourselves," and that's just what the local citizenry did.

Orr's most difficult moments in Oshawa came when he showed up for the first time in the Generals' dressing room. At 14 he was by far the youngest player on the team and his boyish looks accentuated his age. In his own words, he was "scared skinny" when he showed up for training camp.

"I'll never forget that day," said Bobby. "They had a roll call. The players had to call out their names and the position they played. There were some big guys in there and when my turn came, I called my name."

There was a pause and silence filled the room while the 125-pound youngster — smallest in the room — worked up the courage to add his position.

"I said, 'Defense,' and everybody laughed. I guess it was kind of funny at that," Orr smiled. "There I was with all those big guys and me in the middle of them — 14 years old and weighing 125 pounds and claiming I'm a defenseman."

Bobby stared quietly at the floor while coach Doug Williams restored order. A soft-spoken, almost painfully shy youngster, Orr wasn't the type to shake his fist and shout, "I'll show you guys." If he had, he probably would have had a pretty good fight on his hands. That's because his reputation had preceded him to Oshawa. The other General players, all older boys, weren't exactly thrilled over the special privileges being afforded the little kid from Parry Sound. He never had to practice with the team and wasn't subject to the strict curfew that the other players were forced to follow. They had to be in the house by 9 p.m. and in bed by 10.

Who was this shrimp anyway? the other players wondered. He certainly didn't look very special. His crew cut, blond hair emphasized his youthful look and his small build belied his ability. It didn't take long, though, for Orr's teammates as well as his opponents to find out that this 14-year-old could handle himself in the toughest competition.

Like Cinderella arriving in her pumpkin-turned-chariot for the prince's ball, Bobby would show up for every Oshawa game and fit right in with the team offensively and defensively as if he had been practicing with them right along. After the game, he'd dress quickly and rush outside to meet his folks for the long ride home. Sometimes, friends from Parry Sound did chauffeuring for Bobby. Often the job fell to Bob Holmes, owner of Holmes Marina in Parry Sound.

"I first met Bobby when he was a kid playing hockey in our minor system," said Holmes. "But I never really got to know him until he started playing junior in Oshawa and I drove him back and forth."

The conversation on those rides was mostly hockey — both National League and Ontario Junior Hockey Association varieties.

Bobby would replay games over and over with his folks or Holmes, remembering the mistakes he made, and the good plays too. Bobby always was his own severest critic.

The long trip between Oshawa and Parry Sound was made on an average of three times a week, often through snow and sleet storms so much a part of Ontario winters. It was not the very best of arrangements, yet, despite all the travel, Bobby rarely missed school. He kept up his grades in Parry Sound, scored 14 goals in Oshawa, and logged a lot of miles in between the two towns.

Bobby realized that because of his heavy hockey schedule he would have to pay extra attention to his schoolwork to make sure his grades remained acceptable.

Harry Tate, principal of the school Orr attended, called Bobby "a little mischievous at times, like other boys. But he was a good student whom you could trust at any time."

And while Wren Blair was delighted that Bobby had done so well at school under the strain of that year of traveling, he thought about what might have been. When Orr was named to the second all-star team after that first season, Blair sighed.

"Imagine," the Oshawa general manager said, "if he had been able to practice with the team."

There was one game Orr played in his first season which required no travel at all for the tow-headed youngster. In fact, it was his Oshawa teammates who did the traveling while Orr waited for them. Blair had booked an exhibition game for Oshawa against the Parry Sound Shamrocks, an Intermediate B team in Orr's home town. Bobby met his team at his home-town rink.

Bobby's older brother, Ron, played for the Parry Sound team that night, and when a scuffle broke out on the ice, the two Orr brothers found themselves squaring off. "He knocked me down too," said Ron. The final score of the game was Oshawa 11, Parry Sound 3. Bobby Orr had three goals and three assists for the Generals — a productive night — and he didn't have to drive 150 miles to get home after the game.

The early days in Oshawa weren't easy for Bobby. The traveling and some of the resentment from his teammates made things difficult for the 14-year-old. There was one man who made life a little easier, though. He was Stan Waylett, the Oshawa club's trainer.

"He was a second father to me," said Bobby. "At that first training camp in Oshawa, I didn't know where I was or what I was doing. I came into the room and this big bear [Stan] grabbed me and welcomed me to the club."

Waylett was a combination cheer leader, trainer, bus driver, and father confessor for the Oshawa players. And Bobby Orr tapped all of the man's talents. Waylett growled a lot at the players, but underneath he had a warm feeling for them.

"He used to give us a rough time," Orr said. "He would never give us any sticks. I would come in some days and ask for an extra stick and he would say, 'No, you little runt,' and tell me to get out. When I'd come back the night of a game, sure enough, I'd have a new stick."

The hectic schedule of traveling between Oshawa and Parry Sound that first year of junior hockey convinced Arva and Doug Orr that Bobby would be better off boarding in Oshawa for the remainder of his junior career. It is not unusual for local residents in the small towns that dot Canada's countryside to board young hockey players. It is a source of income for the landlords and allows teams to import promising prospects — like Bobby Orr.

The house at 263 Nassau Street in Oshawa was a big shingle building located on a corner. On one side there was a beauty parlor operated by "Bernie" Ellesmere. Bernie and

Bobby was 15 when he moved to Oshawa.

her husband, Bob, are down-to-earth, plain people, much like Arva and Doug Orr.

Their rambling nine-room house gave them more than enough space to board a hockey player or two. "One or two," laughed Mrs. Ellesmere. "One time, there were seven of them in here."

Mike Dubeau, who played for the Generals, had roomed in the Ellesmeres' neighborhood the year before and occasionally baby-sat for the two youngsters in the family, Brian and Frances. It was Dubeau who got the Ellesmere family into the hockey-player boarding business.

"He mentioned us to the club and they asked if we'd take a player," said Bob, who drives a truck for a living. "I said O.K., one. They said, how about two? I agreed." The second player was the shy little defenseman with the blond crew cut.

When Bobby made his first visit to the big house on Nassau Street, he was scared. "I was afraid," he said. "I didn't know what to expect."

What he should have expected and what he got was a family life not unlike the one he had left behind in Parry Sound. The Ellesmeres welcomed Bobby Orr and Mike Dubeau as members of the family. It made things a lot more comfortable for young

Orr, who was experiencing his first separation from his parents, brothers, and sisters.

Bobby Orr was the model boy. "He just stole our hearts away," said Bernie Ellesmere. "Not as a hockey player, but as a boy."

"Both Bobby and Mike worked very hard on their schoolwork," said Bob Ellesmere. "You never had to keep after them about that. Bobby would always be in bed early. Maybe 9 or 9:30. And in the morning, he'd be the first one up."

Young Orr enrolled in R.S. McLaughlin Collegiate High School on the north side of Oshawa, across town from the Ellesmere house. "Sometimes I'd drive him over to the school," said Ellesmere, "and sometimes, he'd walk, just for the exercise. He was always on the go. He could never sit still. I don't remember a single time that he'd sit in the living room and watch a television program from start to finish. Except maybe a hockey game."

Bob Ellesmere was no more than a casual hockey fan until Mike and Bobby invaded his home. "I wasn't a devoted fan," he said. "I'd watch it occasionally. Then when those kids came here, everything changed. I went to every home game."

Bobby gave the Ellesmeres plenty to be proud of — both on the ice and off it. He

Bobby Orr's first roommate at Oshawa was teammate Mike Dubeau.

scored a record-breaking 30 goals for the Generals and delivered more than respectable report cards from school. If anything, the Ellesmeres admit they may have exerted more pressure on Bobby than his parents might have. "We had a certain feeling of responsibility for our hockey players, you know," said Bob. "We made sure they toed the mark."

"The people I lived with in Oshawa — first Bob and Bernie Ellesmere and later Jack and Cora Wild — were harder on us than our parents might have been, I think," said Orr. "But that was natural. They didn't want us to go astray. They were great people, and I was very lucky."

Orr's upbringing in Parry Sound showed in his behavior in Oshawa. "My parents had always taught me to respect other people," said Orr. "I listened to those people and did what they said."

Combining hockey and school wasn't always easy. "We'd practice after school and then there was homework. There wasn't much time for other things," recalled Bobby. Still, he managed to find time for the sort of mischief you might expect from any 15-year-old.

"Once," said Bernie Ellesmere, "around Christmas time, I was very busy in the beauty parlor and I sent Bobby over to the market for some meat. Well, he had that place in a shambles. He had the store manager and all the sales girls over at the meat counter, trying to decide which was the best cut and whether this one was fresh or the other one was fresh. I don't think he wound up buying any of it, but he got a good laugh out of the whole thing."

Another time, Bobby was visiting Joe Bolahood's sporting goods shop on King Street East in Oshawa when the boss sent him out to fetch a hamburger. He should have been suspicious when Bobby showed up with the burger in record time. Bolahood realized why it had come back so fast when he bit into the bun and found that Bobby, the prankster, had inserted a paper napkin where the meat was supposed to be.

No matter where the Oshawa team played, the team always got back to town in time for the players to be at school the next morning. The only exception was when the games were played in Montreal. "Then we'd have to travel all Sunday night and Monday morning to get back in time," said Orr.

The trips were by bus — a far cry from the jet planes that fly National Hockey League teams from coast to coast for their games. Trainer Stan Waylett was the driver and often unpredictable things would take place. "Once we were in a new town," laughed Orr. "Stan said not to worry, that he knew exactly where the rink was. Well, we drove around for three hours before we found it. And it turned out to be only a five-minute drive from where we had started."

In his third year at Oshawa, Bobby moved closer to his school, boarding with Jack and Cora Wild in the red brick house at 331 Walmer Road. The impression he left on the Wilds was no different than the one he had left with the Ellesmeres. "He was wonderful in every way," said Cora Wild.

What was important to the Bruins' organization was that Bobby was just as wonderful on the ice. And the people of Oshawa knew it too.

"We sold out the rink whenever Bobby was playing," said Bill Kurelo, manager of the Oshawa Civic Auditorium. "He was just fabulous."

Kurelo often was alone in his office late in the afternoon when Bobby Orr, the premier defense prospect of all Junior A hockey, would show up early for a game with Jim Whittaker, one of his buddies. Orr would quietly strap on a goaltender's equipment and go into the nets to have Whittaker shoot at him. "The people in Boston would have had

Bobby Orr (front row, third from left) captained the Generals in his final year at Oshawa.

a fit, if they knew about it," said Kurelo, who retained a picture of Bobby making a save, just for proof.

Bobby Orr scored 34 goals in his third season at Oshawa and 38 more in his final junior season. By then, he was 18 and eligible to turn professional with the Bruins. But there was one more stop before that. The Generals, led by the fabulous Orr, who by then had grown into a sturdy 5'11", 180 pounds, weaved their way through preliminary play-offs and into the finals for the cherished Memorial Cup — amateur hockey's equivalent of the NHL's Stanley Cup. But Bobby was suffering from a painful groin injury.

Boston had dispatched general manager Leighton "Hap" Emms to Oshawa to keep an eye on their prize prospect. They didn't want Bobby risking serious, perhaps permanent, injury in his last junior hockey games. But without Orr, Oshawa's chances of beating the Edmonton Oil Kings for the Cup seemed slim.

Doug Orr traveled down from Parry Sound for the final series, just as he had for so many of Bobby's games during his four seasons with the Generals. Doug had made it a practice of letting Bobby do things on his own ever since the younger Orr signed that first agreement linking him to the Bruins four years earlier.

The Generals were trailing in the series three games to two with the sixth game scheduled for Maple Leaf Gardens in Toronto. Doug Orr was inside the Oshawa dressing room, talking to Bobby, who was in obvious pain.

"What do you want to do, son?" asked Doug.

"I want to play," answered Bobby.

"O.K., then, that's it," said Doug. "You go ahead and play."

When the Generals got to the bench, Emms was waiting for the Orrs and Oshawa's coach, Bep Guidolin. "That boy is hurt and he's not to play tonight," the Boston general manager told Guidolin.

"Now just a minute," answered Doug Orr. "He's my son and he wants to play and I say he's going to play."

Bobby Orr played that final game, and although Oshawa lost, 2-1, Doug Orr had established a new kind of relationship with Hap Emms that would become important in the next few months.

"Remember," said the elder Orr to the Boston general manager, "you don't actually own him yet."

Chapter 5

THE SIGNING

THE Boston organization had kept close tabs on Bobby Orr's progress in his four seasons with the Oshawa Generals. And each time the young star did something outstanding, the Bruins made sure the fans on the home front heard about it.

During the four years young Orr was honing his hockey skills in the tough Ontario Hockey Association, the Bruins were suffering through hard times in the National Hockey League. Boston finished next-to-last once and dead-last the other three years of Orr's junior apprenticeship.

Game after game, the Bruins would find imaginative, new ways to lose. Their long-suffering fans would spill out of dreary, drafty old Boston Garden onto Causeway Street, shaking their heads over the team's sorry play. But inevitably the talk would turn to how things were going to be when "that kid . . . you know . . . that kid in Oshawa, Orr, gets here. We'll show them then."

The Bruins were selling Orr to Boston fans four years before he could play for them for a simple reason: Bobby Orr was the best thing the Boston Bruins had to offer — a promise for the future — in those early 1960's.

Indeed, Orr gave the Bruins plenty of ammunition to pass along to the faithful. There were 34 goals and 59 assists in his third year at Oshawa, breaking his own OHA scoring record, and then 37 goals and 60 assists in his final junior season. And as the reports filtered down from Oshawa to Boston, the fans became more and more excited about the sensational young player who was on his way to lead the Bruins back to NHL respectability.

In his final year at Oshawa, Orr was selected along with several other OHA All-Stars to perform against Russia's touring National team in an exhibition game at Maple Leaf Gardens in Toronto. "It was a great experience for me," said Bobby, "to represent my country against the Russians."

That single game would gain significance as the Orr family sat down to talk over Bobby's first professional contract with the Bruins. Hap Emms, Boston's general manager, was dispatched to Oshawa to handle the details and he scheduled a meeting with Bobby and Doug Orr in the Hotel Genosha a few days after their exchange at the final game of the Memorial Cup play-offs.

Doug Orr anticipated some problems with the Bruins. He was sure that the offer the NHL club would make to Bobby and the figure the Orrs had decided to ask for would be far apart. But Bobby's dad decided to take a strong stand in negotiations with the Bruins. The Boston club had been selling Bobby as a million-dollar prospect, and Doug Orr was going to see that they paid his son accordingly. That's why, when Emms and Orr sat down to talk contract, Alan Eagleson, a bright, young Toronto attorney, was waiting in the wings.

Eagleson and Doug Orr had met several years before when both played in the same softball league in Muskoka, Ontario, and they became good friends. The lawyer met young Bobby when the hockey player was only 14 and the two hit it off well together.

"Remember," Eagleson had told Doug Orr, "I'm available if you ever need any help."

Doug Orr remembered the offer and alerted Eagleson as he prepared to sit down with Emms to talk money. The attorney did not enter the negotiations immediately. First, the Orrs wanted to see what the Bruins would offer young Bobby.

Emms was a grandfatherly sort of man who was generous with hockey players as long as it didn't cost money. He produced a standard contract calling for what most hockey players signed for in those days — about $8,000. But Bobby Orr wasn't just another hockey player. Doug Orr knew it and so did Hap Emms.

Emms played it cool at the start of the negotiations. "I can't see any trouble in signing him," Emms said. "He has to prove he can play in this league, then he'll get the big money. I've seen too many of these hotshot juniors who don't make it in the NHL."

Emms, impressed with his own opening argument, picked up steam, pointing out that Bobby Hull had gotten only $8,000; that Gordie Howe had signed in return for a Red Wing warm-up jacket; that Gilles Marotte, another Boston defensive prospect who was also graduating from the junior ranks at that time, had signed a blank contract and was more than happy to have Emms fill in the figures afterward.

If Emms was cool, the Orrs were icy. When Emms realized that Doug and Bobby weren't moving toward that contract, he offered to sweeten the pot. The Bruins' top offer, Emms said, would be a $5,000 bonus and an $8,000 salary. Take it or leave it. Doug Orr left it and indicated to Emms in no uncertain terms that he was totally displeased with the way negotiations had gone. "From now on," Doug Orr told Emms, "Alan Eagleson will handle the negotiations for us."

Eagleson, whom Bobby called "The Eagle," had the Orrs' total trust. The only ones unhappy with Doug Orr's decision to bring Eagleson into the talks were the Bruins. In fact, Emms was more than unhappy. He was upset over the idea of having to negotiate with an attorney and, especially, with *this* attorney. Eagleson, you see, was no stranger to hockey. He represented several Toronto players and already had a reputation as an able and tough negotiator.

The general manager refused to discuss Bobby Orr's contract with this outsider. Emms laid the law down to the Orrs and in no uncertain terms.

All the time that Emms and Doug Orr had argued, Bobby sat back, listening quietly.

He was just 18 and although he was an outstanding hockey player, he never considered himself sophisticated enough to enter into salary negotiations. But now he decided to end his silence.

"Mr. Emms," said Bobby, "either you talk with Mr. Eagleson, or I won't play for the Boston hockey club."

With that, Doug Orr and his son left the room, allowing Emms to soak up Bobby's words by himself. The general manager decided to wait the Orrs out for a little while at least. Tempers had been hot at that initial meeting and Emms wisely thought it best to let everybody cool off. He also made another important decision. He decided that he would, indeed, negotiate with Alan Eagleson.

Emms didn't like to admit it, but Bobby Orr had the Bruins in a rather ticklish position. The Boston club had been selling Orr to its fans for four years. Now it was time to deliver him. If they didn't come through, there was no telling how the Boston faithful might react. As far as Emms and the Bruins were concerned, Bobby Orr had to play for Boston the next year. And if negotiating with Eagleson was the only way to get Orr, well, then Emms would negotiate with Eagleson.

The Toronto attorney was well aware of Boston's predicament. He also had a little ploy of his own. "The National Hockey League," Eagleson told Emms, "isn't the only place Bobby Orr can play hockey. There is the Canadian National team too."

Canada's National team is always shopping for young players. The Nationals can't offer any financial inducements but there are other rewards. Players can continue their education with the government paying tuition. Hockey with the Nationals also offers world-wide travel and the lure of representing Canada in the Olympic Games. It was an idea that appealed somewhat to Bobby Orr and offered excellent ammunition for Eagleson.

Bobby went to work that summer in a boys' camp in Barrie, Ontario, while Eagleson laid the groundwork for serious negotiations with the Bruins by beginning talks with the Canadian Nationals and making certain that Boston heard about the discussions.

Eagleson asked Orr how strongly he wanted to pursue the threat of the National team and Bobby didn't hesitate. "I want to play in the NHL," Orr told the attorney. "But if they don't meet my terms, I won't play there."

It was now August and time was running out for the Bruins. Emms had been adamant in his discussions with Eagleson. "If I give the kid what he wants," Emms argued, "what will I say to my other players?"

And each time Emms said that, Eagleson would counter with: "How many other players have you got with the ability and potential of Bobby Orr?"

The answer was none. That's why, when Eagleson wrote Emms in August setting September 3 as a deadline, the Bruins decided to stop fighting. Training camps would be opening shortly and if Bobby Orr wasn't in Boston's camp, there would be some embarrassing questions that would have to be answered.

So Emms and Eagleson sat down and hammered out most of the details of Bobby's first pro contract. The negotiating was all one way with Emms agreeing to give Bobby just about everything the lawyer asked for. Finally they had the agreement ready and Eagleson called Bobby at the boys' camp.

"Alan asked me to stop by his cottage on my way home," said Bobby. "I used to pass close by to it every day. When I got there, my dad was there along with Alex Eagar and that's when I knew something was up.

Alan said, 'You're going to turn pro tonight.' I was surprised and happy."

The four left Eagleson's cottage and went down to Barrie's harbor where Emms was waiting aboard his 42-foot cabin cruiser, *Barbara Lynn.* It was dark when Orr and his entourage stepped aboard Emms' boat and the scene was illuminated by the Ontario moonlight. And at 1:30 a.m. on September 3, 1966, Bobby Orr signed his contract with the Bruins.

The Bruins have never revealed what they gave Orr. "It's nobody's business," said Emms. But he admitted that he surrendered more than four times his original "best offer." The best guess is that Bobby signed a two-year contract at between $50,000 and $70,000.

When Emms had carefully tucked the document bearing Robert Gordon Orr's signature in a safe spot, he summoned a photographer aboard the boat to record the historic event on film. A mock second signing was staged with Emms posing triumphantly alongside Bobby and his dad.

Next Emms broke out some liquid refreshment to celebrate the occasion. He opened a few bottles of Teem, a grapefruit-flavored beverage, and the signing party finished them off quickly. Then Bobby, his dad, Eagleson, and Alex Eagar left Emm's boat and returned to the attorney's cottage. There they opened a bottle of champagne to toast their victory over the NHL establishment.

As Bobby Orr tasted the bubbly wine for the first time, he began to ponder his first NHL training camp just a few weeks away. He had little time to prepare for his first exposure to the players who would be his new teammates.

Chapter 6

IN TRAINING CAMP
IN LONDON TOWN

THERE was more excitement than usual when the Bruins pitched their training camp in September 1966. The cause of the excitement was an 18-year-old defenseman carrying a fat contract and an enormous amount of publicity.

Each September, the Boston Bruins assemble at camp in London, Ontario, one of the score of small communities that serve as home for the National Hockey League clubs as they get ready for the grueling 70-game season. The small towns look forward to the excitement of hosting major-league athletes for a month or so. And the teams like the atmosphere that creates a feeling of togetherness for their players.

The players spend most of their time with one another during camp. They work out together, eat together, and live together. It forms the basis for the teamwork an NHL club must have to succeed.

"I was a little nervous about the reaction among the Bruins," said Bobby Orr, who wasn't sure just what to expect when he showed up in London. He was, in his own words, "scared skinny," just as he had been four years earlier when he appeared for the first time in the dressing room of the Oshawa Generals.

Orr was assigned to room with Johnny Bucyk, captain of the Bruins and the team's leader on the ice. Bucyk is called "Chief" by his teammates, but Orr didn't think he could take that kind of liberty when he first met his new roomie.

"He walked in the room and I recognized him," said Orr. "He introduced himself and I said, 'Mr. Bucyk, how are you?'"

"Hey," said Bucyk, "watch that 'mister.' It's either Chief or John."

That broke the ice for Bobby. It relaxed him and he wasn't quite so scared skinny any more.

Another time, Orr was leaving his room, carrying a package under his arm, when he bumped into Ron Stewart, a veteran with a peppery sense of humor.

"What's that?" cracked Stewart. "Part of your contract?"

Orr smiled the nervous smile of a young man carrying a rather large burden on his broad shoulders.

When it came time to assign uniform numbers to the rookies on the team, the Bruins were not without a sense of history. They issued Number 4 to Orr — a uniform that fit comfortably into a sequence of retired Boston jerseys, numbers 2, 3, and 5, belonging to the legendary Eddie Shore, Lionel Hitchman, and Dit Clapper. It meant more pressure for the young Orr.

The first day or two in training camp is taken up by check-ins and physical examinations. These over, Bobby Orr paced nervously in his dormitory room, anticipating his first ice time in a Boston uniform.

He couldn't stay in one place for more than a moment. He was full of nervous energy, on the move constantly. Finally, he couldn't take it any more and decided to go down to the rink even though he wasn't due there for some time.

"I always like to get to the rink early," said Orr. But when he arrived at the Bruins' dressing room, there was a surprise waiting

Three rookies: Coach Harry Sinden, flanked by Bobby Orr (left) and Gilles Marotte.

for him. He wasn't the only player there. In fact, he was one of the last to arrive.

His new teammates had arrived early and prepared a little welcome for the rookie defenseman with the fat contract. Spread out in the middle of the dressing room was a blanket.

Orr eyed the blanket quizzically and looked at the other players. "Lay down on it," one of the veterans said solemnly to Orr. "It's a magic blanket. We'll make it rise."

Orr suspected something was up. "But

70

you know," he said later, "I half believed them. I fell into it like a real country huckleberry."

Bobby got down on the blanket and in an instant the Bruins jumped him and pinned him to it. One of the players produced a safety razor and Orr's induction to the Boston hockey club was started.

All rookies brought up to the Bruins experience "The Shave," a rather harrowing initiation ceremony that makes the newcomer one of the boys. "The Shave" is a head-to-toe job done without much concern for the skin of the victim. But it is not done without a studied technique.

"The idea," said goaltender Ed Johnston, "is to loosen the blade of the safety razor enough so it scrapes. Some guys have had 15 or 20 stitches after it's over."

If the ritual sounds scary, that's the idea.

The Bruins ran the razor over Orr from the top of his blond crew-cut up and down his sturdy, well-proportioned body. When they were through, Bobby was well-nicked but more important, he was a member of the team.

Orr held up admirably under the razor. There was some predictable squirming but he quickly realized he'd be better off letting the blade run its course. "It was awful," Bobby said. But when it was over, the only scars the shave left were the physical ones. Orr did not sulk or pout over the rough initiation. He understood it and accepted it and, because he did, he made it easier for the Bruins to understand and accept him.

And when the Bruins saw Bobby on the ice and watched some of the tricks this 18-year-old defenseman could do with a hockey puck, they were just as fascinated as their scouts had been six years earlier in that little rink in Gananoque, Quebec.

Ted Green, Boston's defensive leader until Orr came along, watched the rookie for awhile and then skated over to him. Orr, remembering his initiation by the Boston veterans, wasn't sure what to expect when he saw Green skating toward him. But there was nothing to worry about. Green just had a little message for the high-priced rookie.

"Kid, I don't know what you're getting," said Green, "but it isn't enough."

Orr did all the things in that first Boston camp that he had always done. He stick-handled brilliantly, displayed an amazing skating skill that enabled him to change speed almost as an automobile shifts into overdrive, and had a dazzling command of all of hockey's fundamentals. Still, the Bruins weren't certain just what to do with this fine player in his first professional season.

There was a feeling that all of the publicity surrounding Orr's entrance into the NHL would hurt Bobby. The Bruins knew the other teams were biding their time, preparing to take their best shots at the fuzzy-cheeked rookie. The challenge awed Orr and bothered the Boston club too. In fact, there was some speculation that Boston would ease Bobby's transition from amateur to professional hockey by giving him a year at Oklahoma City in the Central League, one of the top minor leagues.

"I think the people would understand if we decided to do that," said Weston Adams, owner of the club. "Bobby has received a great deal of publicity and in normal cases this might tend to put a lot of pressure on him. But I don't regard Orr as a normal case. He's a mature, level-headed youngster."

Watching the Bruins train that fall, Adams knew that Bobby Orr was far and away the best player the team possessed. There was no way he could be sent to the minors. The Bruins needed him and they needed him right then and there. They needed him so much, in fact, that they couldn't quite decide where Orr would help them most — on defense or at a forward spot.

"I think the boy will be able to adjust to

playing in the NHL at either position," said Adams.

Coach Harry Sinden, an easy-going, friendly man, who, like Orr, was getting his first taste of the NHL, watched Bobby's seemingly endless bag of tricks on the ice and decided it might be worth a try to skate Orr up front for awhile. After all, thought Sinden, he had all the credentials — a strong skater, the quick moves, and a booming shot. So Sinden launched the experiment, skating Orr at center.

"I did what I was told," said Orr, the always obedient and willing youngster. "But I didn't really like it. What I enjoy most about playing defense is that you're facing the play all the time. You can't do that at the other positions. A forward loses the puck, he has to turn and lose sight of what's happening."

Bep Guidolin, Orr's last coach at Oshawa, couldn't understand the experiment that placed his former prodigy up front.

"Orr will be an asset to his team in the NHL," predicted Guidolin. "Bobby's a field general out there, like Doug Harvey. He should be played at the blue line. Up front, they'd check him to death. I'll tell you one thing: he'll be great if he's used on defense and nowhere else."

The experiment employing Orr up front lasted only a short time.

"We stopped using him as a centerman," explained Sinden, "because we decided in a hurry that there's no sense taking the game's best defenseman and playing him at another position. It makes as much sense as playing Elizabeth Taylor in a boy's role."

The position change, the traumatic shave, and the pressure facing any NHL rookie all had their effect on Bobby Orr in his first major-league training camp.

"I didn't know what was missing, what was wrong, when I was here first," said Orr. "I was scared. Scared stiff. I didn't know whether I could make this team. I didn't know whether I could play in the National Hockey League. And I was alone."

As training camp neared its conclusion, Orr's edginess became obvious to some of the older players. Ted Green and Ed Johnston were two who decided to do something about it.

"We could see how uptight he was," said Green. "We tried to make it easier for him."

Orr and Gary Doak, another rookie defenseman, were virtually adopted by Green, Johnston, and John Forristall, the team's assistant trainer.

"They became our family and our

friends," said Orr. "They made camp like home and they made sure we kept in touch with home."

Immediately, Orr's new-found family brightened the youngster up. Camp was almost like being back in Parry Sound with all his friends and neighbors. When the Bruins began to close camp, Orr and Doak decided to try and maintain the close-knit feeling their friendship with Green and Johnston had created.

"When we were breaking camp, Bobby and Gary asked me what plans I had when we got back to Boston," said Johnston, who, unlike Green, was a bachelor. "I told them I'd always had a place of my own. I said I'd probably move back into my own apartment. They said they were going to take a place and they asked me if I'd like to move in with them. Since they asked me, I figured it was O.K. and I said yes."

Orr, Doak, Johnston, and Forristal, the trainer, moved into a three-bedroom house in Nahant, a suburb of Boston. It was a big, friendly house, not unlike the one Bobby grew up in at Parry Sound or the ones he boarded in at Oshawa. There were always people around — a lot of laughter and a lot of fun. It was the kind of atmosphere in which Bobby Orr had always flourished.

Chapter 7

THE ROOKIE

"I'VE never been so nervous in my life," said Bobby Orr. "This was my big night. This was what I was waiting for. The NHL."

The Bruins opened their schedule at home, hosting the Detroit Red Wings in the opening game at ancient Boston Garden. The date was October 19.

The 1966-67 season was to mark the 50th anniversary of the National Hockey League and its final year as a six-team league. For 24 years, the league had operated with six clubs: New York, Boston, Montreal, Toronto, Detroit, and Chicago. But plans had already been approved for an ambitious expansion that would double the league's size

to 12 teams the next season and grant new franchises to St. Louis, Philadelphia, Pittsburgh, Oakland, Los Angeles, and Minneapolis-St. Paul.

The anticipation of the following year's expansion kept NHL officials busy all through the 1966-67 season, but not too busy to overlook the young man breaking in on defense for the Boston Bruins. Everyone wanted to see what Bobby Orr was all about.

The excitement charged through Orr's body like electricity. He slept fitfully the night before the game and got up early that morning, busying himself around the house he now shared with teammates Ed Johnston and Gary Doak.

"I was very excited," said Orr. "I couldn't wait for the game."

At about 4:30 or 5 o'clock in the afternoon, the crew-cut rookie defenseman showed up at the Bruins' dressing room. He had 3½ hours to wait for game time but this was one game he wasn't going to be late for.

The only person in Boston Garden that night who was as nervous as Orr was Boston coach Harry Sinden, who, like Bobby, was making his NHL debut. Sinden started Orr on defense.

"Bobby was a star," Sinden said, "from

the moment they played the 'National Anthem' in that first game."

The Bruins won the opener 6-2, and Bobby Orr assisted on one of the goals scored by his training-camp roommate, Johnny Bucyk.

After the game, the hero-starved Boston writers surrounded Orr in the Bruin dressing room. "That was a heckuva play you made on that goal," one of them said.

"Thank you," said the polite defenseman, chuckling to himself.

"What had happened," Orr said later, "was that I had the puck at the blue line and I went to shoot. But I fanned on the shot and the puck just slid over to the Chief and he put it in. I guess it looked like I was passing the puck, but I wasn't. I was shooting for the net. I just missed."

No matter what his intentions had been, Bobby Orr had his first NHL point. Four nights later, he earned his first goal and this one was no mistake.

The Montreal Canadiens were in Boston Garden for the second game of a home-and-home series between the two clubs. Gump Worsley, the grizzled veteran goalie, was in the nets for the Canadiens. The Bruins buzzed into Montreal's end of the ice and three forwards swarmed around the Canadiens' net while Orr set himself up at the

Bobby Orr learned many tricks of the trade in
his rookie year in the NHL.

point, just inside the blue line. Worsley frantically dove and flopped, blocking the puck once, twice, three times.

Finally the disc found its way out to Orr, waiting patiently at the point. Bobby wound up and his stick caught the puck perfectly. The rubber flew toward Worsley, seemingly picking up speed as it neared the net. It was only a blur as it whipped past the goalie. Bobby Orr had scored.

The roar of the Boston crowd seemed to build, section by section, until the old building that stands atop North Station seemed to shake. All that the fans had been fed about Orr for four years was true. He was a super hockey player and he was proving it to some of hockey's toughest critics — the Boston fans.

Doug Orr was in the stands that night in Boston Garden and a chill ran up and down his spine as the fans' cheers cascaded through the arena. Even Toe Blake, the veteran coach of the Canadiens, was amazed at the response of the fans. "I never heard anything like it," said Blake, who once was a linemate of Maurice Richard's and had heard some deafening ovations for the Rocket's feats.

Orr's teammates fished the puck out of the Montreal net and made sure he got it as a souvenir of the memorable event. Bobby passed it along to his father, who would later have the puck mounted and engraved in gold.

So, within a space of three games, Bobby Orr had his first NHL goal and his first NHL assist. But life in hockey's big league isn't always that pleasant.

The hatchetmen were waiting eagerly for Orr, anxious to test the baby-faced prodigy from Parry Sound. They gave Bobby the business, but good.

"I learned a young player can't stand around watching where a pass goes once he makes it," said Orr. "It's a good way to end up in the first row."

Orr never wound up among the paying customers but he came close a couple of times. In a game in Toronto, Orr emerged with a purple welt across his mid-section after being speared by defenseman Kent Douglas. Detroit's all-time scoring champ, Gordie Howe, introduced Bobby to "the two-hander" which is a rap across the gloves that is not especially good for the hands.

There were bouts with New York's Reg Fleming and Montreal's Ted Harris, considered one of the best fighters in the NHL. Orr knocked Harris down twice, a fact that amused New York's Orland Kurtenbach,

Tough guys like New York's Reggie Fleming
(9) constantly put Bobby Orr to the test.

another heavyweight who engaged Orr early in that first season.

"Did he really knock Harris down?" asked Kurtenbach.

Assured that Orr had done just that, Kurtenbach laughed. "The kid's got good balance. He's hard to knock off his pins."

Throughout that first year, Orr remembered some advice that he'd gotten from Wren Blair, the man who originally signed him when he was 14 years old.

"Don't back up," Blair told Bobby. "There are gonna be players who'll resent you. When that happens, throw off your gloves and go at them. Let them know right away where you stand. There are darn few players who really want to fight. If you show them you want to fight, they'll get the message in a hurry. Get it over with so that you're not hampered by that nonsense too long. Then let your hockey ability take over."

"I don't look for fights," said Orr, "but I don't back down from them either."

Bobby Orr's initiation into life in the NHL had plenty of difficult moments — moments that were very embarrassing, to say the least. There was one game in New York when Bobby started a rush out of the Boston zone. He crossed into center ice, employing one of what teammate Ted Green likes to call his "18 speeds of fast." Then he heard a voice behind him shouting, "Drop it, Bobby, drop it."

Figuring he'd set up a teammate for a better shot at the Ranger net, Orr obediently dropped the puck. He pulled up and wheeled around just in time to see New York's Vic Hadfield, the mysterious voice from behind, pick up the puck and return it to Boston's zone.

Another night, Montreal's John Ferguson, hardly a graceful skater, shoveled the puck through Orr's legs and went right around the defenseman for a clean shot on net. But in Boston, Orr could do no wrong. One leather-lunged fan reacted to the rookie's mistake by shouting, "Westfall you bum, get off the ice." Poor Ed Westfall, another Bruin defenseman, was on the bench at the time. Nobody wanted to blame Orr for anything.

In another game, Orr had a nightmarish night. He was on the ice for five goals by the opposition and directly responsible for the first three. But he never heard a boo all game long.

"He could be on the ice for 15 goals," said Harry Sinden, his coach. "He could score five goals in our own net and the crowd wouldn't get on him. He's just too

good most of the time. He gets caught sometimes, but it's only because, when we're
losing a game, he takes it on his shoulders
to tie it or win it for us. If we're down two
goals in the second period, he wants to take
the puck and score a goal. That way, he isn't
always in good command of his position.
We're always playing catch-up hockey, so it
places that much more pressure on him."

Orr's individual brilliance was not enough
by itself to improve Boston's standing in the
league. The Bruins still struggled along near
the bottom and the fans often blistered general manager Hap Emms. One patron shouted
at him, "Hey Emms, why don't you trade
Orr? He's making the rest of the Bruins
look bad."

Off the ice, Orr was a typical teenager.
He always had something going on in the big
house in Nahant and, all of a sudden, staying
at home didn't seem so bad to bachelor goalie
Ed Johnston, one of Bobby's roomies.

"We'd have card tournaments and checker tournaments and talk about hockey," said
Johnston. "We'd yell and scream and unwind
a lot. It's all in fun and it breaks up the
evening. Pretty soon, it's 11 o'clock and you
feel like going to bed. I bet I didn't go
downtown 10 times all season."

Bobby would always be the first one up in

the morning and he usually had a pot of coffee going by the time the others came down on the way to practice.

On game days, Bobby and the Bruins eat their big meal, usually a steak, about 1 p.m. "Bobby could eat three or four steaks a day," said Johnston. "If I ate the way he does, I'd weigh about 250 pounds. But he never has trouble with his weight."

After the steak — medium, please — Orr takes a nap until about 3:30. Then he's up and, before too long, he's on his way to the rink, even though the game may be as many as four hours away. He gives all kinds of excuses for getting to the rink so early, but mostly he simply wants to be alone for awhile, to think about the job ahead of him, and to get his mind off everything else except the night's game.

After the game, Orr often has a date for dinner. Occasionally, he and his roommates have a gathering at their house in Nahant.

"We'll talk about the game and relax," said Johnston. "You try to keep it small. Sometimes Bobby will say, 'I shouldn't have let that guy get past me,' things like that. But mostly he's real quiet."

Orr let his performance on the ice do his talking for him in that first year with the Bruins. Bobby scored 13 goals and assisted on 28 others for 41 points, third best total on the team. He also accumulated 102 penalty minutes, pushing back whenever an opponent decided to test his taste for fighting.

The performance earned Orr the Calder Trophy as the NHL's best rookie that season. He also was named to the second All-Star team — quite an accomplishment for an 18-year-old. ?

Perhaps the most eloquent commentary on Orr's rookie season came from Harry Howell, a veteran of 15 seasons on defense for the New York Rangers. Howell had enjoyed his finest year in 1966-67 and was awarded the Norris Trophy as the premier defenseman in the league. A big grin creased his face as Howell stepped forward at the presentation ceremony to accept the treasured Norris award.

"I'm sure glad I won this thing this year," said Howell, "because from now on, I've got a feeling that it's going to belong to Bobby Orr."

Chapter 8

CRUTCHES
AND ALL

HIS first National Hockey League season a happy memory, Bobby Orr returned to Parry Sound for a carefree summer. There would be fishing, hunting, and some plain, old-fashioned loafing.

The solitude of Parry Sound was enticing to Orr after the hustle and bustle of his first season with the Bruins. Yet, he had been a little worried about returning home.

"I was almost afraid to go back to Parry Sound," said Orr. "You know how it is . . . you're walking along the street and don't happen to notice someone. The next thing you know, word gets around that 'Orr has gone snooty on us. He doesn't even say hello to his home-town people any more.' I thought maybe I'd just disappear and go fishing."

Orr's fears were unfounded, simply because he never overlooked any of his friends in Parry Sound. If he knew you before he reached the NHL, he still knew you afterward. Success had not changed Bobby Orr.

The only difference between his first summer home after his rookie season with the Bruins and previous summers in Parry Sound was the increased demands on his time. There were dinners and appearances overcrowding the schedule that Bobby ordinarily would fill with his summertime activities. But Orr was an NHL star now and there were more and more requests for his time. Sometimes Bobby yearned for those earlier years when his time was his own.

One of his appearances in the summer of 1967 was scheduled for Winnipeg, Manitoba, where a group of NHL players were performing in a benefit game against the Canadian National team. There were two lures concerning the invitation that Orr couldn't resist. One was that the Canadian National team — a club close to Orr's heart after he had used it in negotiations with Hap Emms for his first pro contract — was involved. The other was that it was a benefit game, something that would help those not as for-

tunate as Orr. Bobby rarely turned down a
charity appeal, and when Jim Dunn, president of the Manitoba Oldtimers' Association,
tended the invitation, Bobby quickly accepted.

Around the time that Orr was getting settled for his summer, there was an executive
shake-up in Boston. Owner Weston Adams
replaced his general manager, Hap Emms,
with long-time Bruin favorite, Milt Schmidt.
Emms had trouble getting along with the
players — the Orr-signing crisis was one of
the problems that led to his eventual dis-
missal. Schmidt, on the other hand, was a
younger man whose Hall of Fame member-
ship and outstanding playing record earned
the respect of all the athletes.

In another move, veteran NHL defenseman Tom Johnson, who had been on the
Bruin payroll as a scout for a couple of seasons after an eye injury ended his playing
career, was moved in as an assistant to
Adams.

Both shifts were important because when
Dunn got Orr's acceptance to play in the
Manitoba charity game, he decided to check
with the Bruins' front office. "I called Boston and got verbal permission from Johnson," Dunn said.

A few weeks after that fateful conversation, Schmidt was out on a golf course, practicing his drives and putts, when he was interrupted by an urgent phone call. Bobby Orr, the message said, was in a Manitoba hospital with strained ligaments in his right knee, suffered in some kind of benefit hockey game.

Schmidt's blood pressure rose a few points when he got the report. The Bruins' general manager had no idea that his prized property was in Manitoba at all, no less playing hockey games.

"It was a sheer accident," explained Orr. "A guy steered me into the boards and another guy, who was on my side, hit me."

The explanation hardly satisfied Schmidt.

"NHL contracts specify that a player must have written permission to appear in those kind of games," said Schmidt, "and Orr did not have it."

Dunn, meanwhile, insisted that Tom Johnson knew all about the game and had given the go-ahead. And Orr couldn't see what the Bruins were so excited about.

"After all," Bobby said, "it was a benefit for old-time hockey players."

The injury in the Manitoba benefit game was a bad omen for Orr. It cost him five weeks in a cast and was only the first in an

Bobby Orr went down in a heap, his nose broken.

annoying line of accidents that severely limited his production for the Bruins.

Because of his talent and the obvious fact that the Bruin attack depended on Orr's ability to move the puck, enemy defenders set their sights on Bobby. Anytime they could line Orr up for a shot, they did it and before too long, Bobby started belting back.

The season was less than one month old when the Toronto Maple Leafs came into Boston Garden for a game against the Bruins. Brian Conacher, latest member of the great Canadian hockey-playing family to make it to the NHL, was skating on one of the Leafs' forward lines. Midway through the game, Conacher crashed into Orr and Bobby went down in a heap, his nose broken.

As Orr scrambled to his feet, he felt the blood running down the side of his mouth. Conacher's stick had broken his nose and cut him as well, and the sight of his own blood sent Bobby into a frenzy. He chased Conacher all over the ice and when he finally caught up with the Toronto forward, Bobby tore into him with both fists pumping away like pistons.

It was a one-way fight with Orr pummeling away at Conacher, beating a steady tattoo on the whipped Leaf. Sometime during the pummeling, Orr injured a thumb and, after serving his penalty for the fight, Bobby was able to take only one more turn on the ice, not because of his broken nose but because of the bruised thumb. The episode left Orr bitter.

"Conacher got me in the nose," Bobby said, "and frankly, I didn't want to fight. But if they see you backing up in this league, it's no good. So, if they want to fight, I'll fight."

Still, that didn't explain the fury with which Orr turned on Conacher. "He hit me with his stick," said Orr, gritting his teeth. "I didn't like that. A guy can beat me with his fists and I won't complain, but not with the stick. I hate sticks."

Still, the Conacher fight showed that Orr could be provoked into taking himself out of a game on penalties. The Bruins' front office recognized that other teams might zero in on Bobby, foul him, and hope that he retaliated and drew penalties for his actions. Orr, they reasoned, couldn't set up plays and score goals from the penalty box.

"After the Conacher incident," said Schmidt, "I had a talk with Bobby. I told him he could avoid such things as that. I can understand his feelings." But the message was that Orr's feelings had to be contained as best Bobby could contain them.

Shortly after his bout with Conacher, another Toronto player, veteran defenseman Marcel Pronovost, evened the score with Orr, nailing him with a clean body check that sent him banging into the boards. As Orr bounced into the herculite glass that surrounds the rink, he felt his knee go.

When an athlete's knee is damaged, it's like the hinge of a door suddenly collapsing, with no means of support. Bobby limped off the ice and was hospitalized. He spent 10 days off the leg before the Bruins' doctors gave him the green light to resume skating.

But now there was a question about Orr's legs. His knees had been seriously damaged twice inside of a few months and even Orr was wondering how much punishment they could take.

The preoccupation with protecting his knees left the rest of Orr's body open to shots and he absorbed some good ones. In December trouble struck again, with Toronto the foe once more. The Maple Leafs' Frank Mahovlich leveled Bobby with a resounding body check. Orr went down in a heap and had to be helped off the ice. The diagnosis was a fractured collarbone and it was later discovered that he had also suffered a shoulder separation in the mishap. Again it meant taking his hockey from the sidelines, something

Bobby Orr had always found most difficult. Because he never liked to be out of the line-up, it worked against him. He would try to play despite bumps and bruises and sometimes aggravated injuries because he preferred to neglect them.

"I've never seen him when he isn't trying to live up to his reputation," said Harry Sinden. "What this means is that he won't tell anyone when he's injured. Unless you catch him off guard or some bones are broken, you never know if he's hurt. All he ever says is, 'I'm all right, I'm all right.'"

Perhaps Orr shrugged off injuries because they had never really bothered him until now. In his four seasons of junior hockey at Oshawa, he had accumulated only 22 stitches, a low number for a hockey player.

"Stitches like mine," Bobby said, "are just Band-Aid stuff so far. You know I've still got all my teeth, but I don't want people to think I'm bragging about it."

Despite his early-season bumps and bruises, Orr had emerged as one of the finest defensemen in the league and he was selected to play in the mid-season All-Star Game at Toronto's Maple Leaf Gardens.

Toe Blake, coaching Orr's team, played Bobby just the way his regular coach, Harry Sinden, had — using him as much as he could. Suddenly, Pete Stemkowski of the Maple Leafs caught Orr with a solid check, bouncing him into the boards. Bobby's wince was an immediate tip-off to Sinden and Milt Schmidt that their wonder boy was hurt. "But he felt he had to live up to the honor of being an All-Star," said Sinden.

Schmidt rushed down behind the bench and shouted at Blake to remove Orr from the game. But Blake didn't realize Bobby was hurt and, at that particular moment, the blond defenseman from Boston was the All-Stars' best man on the ice.

After the game, it was discovered that Stemkowski's check had damaged Orr's shoulder again, just as Sinden and Schmidt had suspected. "I hardly noticed it while I was playing," said Orr, "but later in the night, I had trouble lifting my arm."

The shoulder cost Orr five more games. He was barely back in the line-up when his old knee problem cropped up again. This time it happened in a game against St. Louis and it was his left knee.

Bobby tried to ignore it but the hockey grapevine was buzzing that the Boston star was injury-prone, that he was brittle.

"It's something I'll have to get used to," said Orr. "People tell me I'm brittle, but I can't afford to think things like this. I won't let it affect my play. I only wish there was a 'Brittle Test' so I could know once and for all what the story is."

A few days after the St. Louis game, his knee broke down again. The Bruins were in Detroit for a game against the Red Wings and, as soon as Orr stepped on the ice, his left knee went on him. Schmidt hustled Bobby back to Boston for a complete examination.

"The knee locks up on him," the worried general manager explained. "It's been getting worse. When he lifts his leg and tries to skate, the joint sticks and it won't come back easily."

On February 10, 1968, Orr flew into Boston's Logan Airport and for the first time since he'd come to the NHL, his happy, carefree teenage disposition was replaced by a deep concern — concern not only for the throbbing pain in his left knee but also for his future in the NHL.

He hurried through the terminal, answering reporters' questions with a curt, "I just don't know. Please, I just don't want to talk about it."

Two days later, Dr. Ronald Adams, the Bruins' club physician, and Dr. Robert George, an orthopedic specialist, operated on

Orr's left knee in Newton Wellesley Hospital. After the operation, the doctors held a press conference that would have been worthy of a Presidential patient.

"Orr suffered a rather classic bucket handle tear of the medial meniscus," said Dr. George, explaining that the meniscus is the outer cartilage of the knee, a narrow, crescent-shaped padding. "It was rather comparable to the removal of an appendix."

"The operation was completely successful," said Dr. Adams, "and badly needed."

When Orr appeared before the press a few days later, he was in a wheelchair, his left knee encased in a huge cast. One look at the calendar, which showed just six weeks left to the regular season, and one look at that huge cast led to the simple conclusion that there would be no more hockey for Bobby Orr in the 1967-68 season. But that was the logical conclusion and logic does not take into consideration the drive of a hockey player whose team is involved in a battle for first place.

Orr, still one month short of his 20th birthday began a rehabilitation program to rebuild his leg. He spent hours day after day lifting weights with the leg and riding a stationary bicycle to strengthen the knee. The doctors were impressed by his program

UPI

A few days after his knee operation, Orr came
to a press conference in a wheelchair.

and the positive reports from the hospital kept the Bruins going. Boston was involved in a tough battle with Montreal, New York, and Chicago; and an early return by Orr would be a tremendous boost for the club.

Bobby was rushing nature a bit. But on March 12, exactly one month after the operation, he laced on a pair of skates for a light workout to see just how much pressure the damaged knee could support.

The workout was held in empty Boston Garden and, just as they had so often in the past, top officials of the club gathered to watch Orr skate. The scene brought to mind the bantam game in Gananoque where Orr was first discovered and at the tryout camp in Niagara Falls when Bruin officials decided they could wait no longer for the young defenseman.

Orr stepped carefully onto the frozen surface, looking more like a hockey novice than an NHL All-Star. He moved easily around the rink, slowly but surely working out the kinks brought on by one month in a hospital bed.

"I was anxious," Orr admitted. "I was also a little worried about how I'd feel. It's like going into your first game. You just turn easy and slow."

All Orr needed was a little time to recover

his full mobility. The Bruins gave him two more weeks and on March 24, after missing 17 games, they returned him to the line-up for a game against Detroit.

Orr was uptight before the game and it showed in his performance on the ice. "I just don't know how I'm going to feel after this one," he said before taking the ice. "It's like a guy going into his first game."

In the second period, Orr got into an argument with referee Bill Friday. When Bobby seemed to bring his hands up to his throat in the choke-up sign so provocative to all sports officials, Friday tagged him with the first misconduct. Bobby stormed to the penalty box and slammed the door violently behind him, right in the referee's face. That earned him the second misconduct.

"Bill, I didn't know you were there," Orr said, explaining the door-slamming. "And if I did, I'd have slammed it harder than that." The Bruins lost the game 5-3.

Despite Orr's return to the line-up, the Bruins were beaten out of the top two spots in the standings by Montreal and New York. Boston, however, was more than happy to settle for third place — the Bruins' first play-off berth in nine years. The fact that they would meet the powerful Canadiens in the opening Stanley Cup play-off round hardly seemed to matter.

But what did matter was that Orr did not seem himself on the ice. He wasn't as mobile as the Bruins had remembered him. It seemed that the knee might still be bothering the young defenseman.

The Canadiens picked the Bruins apart, eliminating Boston in four straight games. They contained Orr almost completely, limiting him to two meager assists. Bobby insisted that there was nothing wrong with his knee but that kind of denial was old stuff to Bruin officials.

The knee did bother Bobby and in early June he went to see Dr. John Palmer, a Toronto surgeon. Sure enough, Dr. Palmer found a cartilage chip in the knee and once again, Orr was ordered onto an operating table.

"Bobby simply aggravated his condition," Dr. Palmer explained. "The first operation was to remove a piece of cartilage already torn. Today's surgery was simply to remove a small chip. Bobby won't have any problem with the knee in the future."

Orr was still on crutches shortly afterward when the NHL's annual awards were announced. He was stunned to find that, in a season in which he missed 28 games because of his succession of injuries, he had been elected to the first All-Star team and been awarded the Norris Trophy as the league's outstanding defenseman. He earned the two honors with 11 goals and 20 assists in just 46 games.

Bobby just shook his head when he heard about the awards. "They gave me the Norris Trophy, but I didn't deserve it," he said. "I only played, what, 46 games? I had a bad play-off and, all in all, I thought I had a terrible year."

Then Orr glanced at the cast on his leg again and wondered what he had done to earn the trophy. It might have been more appropriate, thought Bobby, for the voters to award him a purple heart.

Chapter 9

BIG MONEY

WHEN he took over as general manager of the Bruins in 1967, Milt Schmidt took one look at his team's roster and decided he knew what was wrong with the club. The players were simply too small. One day Schmidt was discussing the plight of the team with some of his scouts. He pointed to the door.

"I want players who can't fit through there," the general manager said. And then he went about the task of assembling athletes who fit that description.

Perhaps the single most significant move in changing the character of the Bruins was a six-player trade which Schmidt negotiated with Chicago. The deal cost the Bruins very little and brought them three solid hockey players.

In the trade, Schmidt surrendered Pit Martin, a smallish center; Gilles Marotte, a defenseman still rough around the edges; and Jack Norris, a minor-league goalie. In exchange, he got centers Phil Esposito and Fred Stanfield and right winger Ken Hodge.

Esposito had been Bobby Hull's center at Chicago and was completely overshadowed by the Golden Jet. Stanfield and Hodge were young players who had played part-time for the Black Hawks. The key to the trade was size. Esposito and Hodge were both big and strong and contrasted Martin who stood only five-foot-eight and weighed 160 pounds.

Freed from the responsibility of setting up Hull, Esposito blossomed into a top scorer in Boston. Using his size to plant himself in front of enemy nets, the big guy produced 35 goals, 49 assists, and 84 points — second best total in the NHL. It was 25 points more than Esposito's best previous NHL performance.

Given the right-wing job on Esposito's line, Hodge also produced handsomely, coming up with 25 goals, 31 assists, and 56 points. Stanfield, pivoting another line, had 20 goals, matching the total Martin had

UPI

Phil Esposito (right) gave Bobby Orr and the
Boston Bruins added scoring punch.

given the Bruins the year before. So Schmidt added 60 goals up front as a result of the big trade.

Another new face vital to the success of the Bruins was a dead-end kid up from Niagara Falls named Derek Sanderson. He centered the Bruins' other line and pitched in with 24 goals, 25 assists, and 49 points. The performance earned him the Calder Trophy as Rookie of the Year — the award that Bobby Orr had won the year before.

Two veteran forwards, John McKenzie and Johnny Bucyk, both had their best seasons ever. McKenzie, a journeyman making his fourth NHL stop, had 28 goals, 38 assists, and 66 points, while Bucyk produced 30 goals, 39 assists, and 69 points — a career high in his 13th NHL season.

On defense, Boston had added tough Don Awrey, who was limited to four games in Orr's rookie season the year before but played the full 74-game schedule in 1967-68, and Dallas Smith, a belter who was overmatched as a 19-year-old rookie six years before but had gained maturity and added depth to the defense.

Another deal that grew out of Schmidt's desire for size sent slightly built Murray Oliver to Toronto for the sturdier Eddie Shack. That one paid off too with Shack adding 23 goals to the Bruins' attack, 14 more than Oliver had scored the year before.

All of the added goals made the Bruins the highest-scoring team in the league. They totaled 259 goals in 1967-68, 14 more than their nearest rivals, the Detroit Red Wings. But the Wings finished last in the East and Boston was third. The difference was defense and that's where Bobby Orr was the key.

Despite all of his injuries and limited action, Orr had emerged as the defensive leader of the Bruins. That's why the summer of 1968 was so important to both Boston and Bobby. It was during that summer that Orr had to recover from his second major knee operation. The recovery had to be mental as well as physical and it was not easy.

After Orr returned home following his injury-filled season, the town of Parry Sound decided to honor him. A few days before his second operation, Parry Sound celebrated Bobby Orr Day and packed all of its pride into a giant testimonial to the young defenseman.

Several of Orr's teammates traveled to the northern Ontario town to join in the celebration and there were players from other teams as well, including Gary Sabourin of the St. Louis Blues, who, like Orr, had grown up and developed in Parry Sound.

"I want to thank the sponsors of this program," Sabourin said, "for giving me the opportunity to see Bobby Orr . . . standing still."

The audience roared over Sabourin's crack and Orr just smiled his boyish grin. In the back of his mind, he wondered whether his bad knee would keep him standing still forever.

"Maybe I don't show it," said Orr, "but I worry. About my health and my legs."

The Bruins, of course, were worried too. Not only about Bobby's legs, but about his new contract. The original two-year pact he had signed with Hap Emms had expired and Alan Eagleson, Orr's talented attorney, was ready to negotiate a new one. But first there was the operation to worry about.

Dr. John Palmer removed the chips in mid-June and Orr spent the next eight weeks on crutches. Part of his rehabilitation during that period involved lifting weights with his leg and riding a stationary bicycle. He underwent whirlpool treatments two and three times a week. This program was becoming routine for Orr, who had been through the same thing only four months earlier following his first operation.

Dr. Palmer kept a close eye on Bobby's progress and seemed completely satisfied, even if Orr wasn't. After all, what 20-year old wants to spend his summer vacation on a pair of crutches? Day after day, Orr followed the regimen prescribed by the doctor and slowly the knee responded.

Finally, in September, Dr. Palmer was satisfied enough with his patient's progress to give young Orr a little treat.

"O.K., Bob," the doctor said, "you can get rid of the crutches any time now."

Orr couldn't wait to get back to Parry Sound with the good news. Those crutches weren't going to be just tossed out casually. No sir. The people of Parry Sound had special plans for them.

Orr and his crutches were invited to an old-fashioned cookout to be held in a secluded corner of land at the edge of the Georgian Bay. There were the usual cookout goodies but the highlight of the evening was a ceremonial sacrifice.

"A whole bunch of people came out," said Orr, "and burned my crutches to a crisp."

It was quite a scene. There were Orr's crutches, the very things that enabled Bobby to get from place to place all summer, going up in smoke and most of Parry Sound cheering their destruction. And while they cheered the crutch-burning, the people all said a silent prayer it would be the last time

Bobby would have to worry about crutches.

While Orr busied himself rebuilding his knee, Eagleson spent his summer talking contract terms with the Bruins. He approached the problem eagerly. "Bobby proved in just two years that he is now the greatest player in the Bruins' history," the lawyer said. And he set out to see to it that his client was paid appropriately.

Remembering the scars of his summerlong squabble with Hap Emms two years before, Eagleson readied himself for another bitter bout with the Bruins' front office. Surprisingly, it never really developed.

"The negotiations were long," the attorney said, "but fairly easy. The Bruins knew what Bobby was worth and they were quite reasonable."

Quite reasonable by Eagleson's definition was a three-year contract that carried six figures and made Bobby Orr, at the age of 20, the highest-paid player in NHL history.

The figure mentioned most frequently for the three years was $400,000 — a staggering amount when you consider that, until Orr arrived in the NHL, the top salary in the league was reported to be the $50,000 or so a season that Gordie Howe was earning from Detroit. And Howe was in his third NHL season in 1948 when Orr was born.

The numbers caused shock waves all around the NHL. Other players looked at the figure logically. "I think I'm half as good as Bobby Orr," reasoned his teammate, Ed Westfall. "Maybe I can get half as much money."

The Bruins quickly denied the $400,000 figure, claiming it was greatly inflated over what Bobby had actually received.

"I don't care if the story was wrong," said veteran Henri Richard of the Montreal Canadiens. "It should help us all. I don't see why we don't get paid as much as the baseball or football players anyway."

Howe, in the middle of a two-year contract, was impressed by Orr's numbers. "I don't think he's actually getting all that kind of money," said hockey's all-time scoring champ. "But don't kid yourself; a lot of guys will have news clippings of Orr's contract-signing when they talk to the boss this year. I'm going to mention it."

The Wings renegotiated Howe's contract and rewarded him with an $80,000 agreement. But the Chicago Black Hawks weren't quite so co-operative with their star, Bobby Hull. Hull got into a long-term battle with Black Hawk officials over terms of his contract and finally stunned the hockey world by announcing his retirement from the sport — a premature retirement when one considers that, at 29, he was at the peak of his productive years.

When the Hawks realized that Hull was serious about quitting, they came to a meeting of the minds with their strapping left winger and he agreed to return. It was reported that his return was based on a contract that matched Orr's.

The Boston star was bothered by all of the excitement created by his contract.

"I never said what I signed for," said Orr. "And I don't think it's right for people to write what they think I signed for. I don't know or even want to know how much writers make. I don't know why they should know what I make. I wouldn't go up to another fellow and ask him what he makes. And I think I'm entitled to the same thing."

The thing about all of the excitement surrounding his salary was that it excited the rest of the hockey world a lot more than it did Orr. Bobby is more concerned with how well he plays hockey rather than how much he gets paid for it.

"He'll think nothing of carrying checks around in his pocket for months," said Eagleson, who doubles as Orr's financial advisor as well as his attorney. "He gave me a check in June that he had in his pocket since January 18. It was for $11,000. I think one reason for this is that a part of him doesn't want to have this kind of money because it sets him apart from his teammates, and that's the one thing he hates most in the world. That's the one thing he'll fight you about, if you set him up as something apart from the team. He's the best team man there ever was."

When Orr signed his contract there were some problems among the Bruins' players. Defenseman Ted Green wanted to renegotiate his pact and wound up walking out of the club's training camp when the team refused.

"I'd rather give those players my money," said Orr, "than have any of that unhappiness; that is, if there is any. I don't know if there is or was any. If there is, I'd just as soon not know about it. But I haven't seen any evidence of it; in fact, all the guys on the team have been super to me."

Green sat tight, almost until the opening of the season, then changed his mind and returned to the team. His holdout meant that the club had gone through training camp without two of its best defensemen. Green was in Manitoba and Bobby Orr was on the sidelines, resting his still bothersome and now quite expensive left knee.

Chapter 10

A RECORD TUNE

BOBBY Orr stood at the sideboards, near the bench, as the Bruins opened their training camp for the 1968-69 season. He took a deep breath, grasped the boards, and stepped gingerly onto the ice, digging the blades of his skates carefully into the ice, listening for the familiar crunch of steel against frozen surface.

Orr glided easily around the rink in London, Ontario, shifting his weight from one side to the other, stepping into each stride a bit more determinedly than the one before. Skating was never an effort for the talented young defenseman, but as he moved easily around the ice, he seemed disturbed.

His moves were labored, not as smooth and as graceful as they had been in the past. It was clear that his knee was not right.

Bobby tried to ignore the problem, shrugging off inquiries, saying, "I know there are some people who say I'm injury-prone. There's nothing I can do about that. The knee? Oh, it's O.K. I'm anxious to get some contact work."

But the knee was not all right. There was pain and swelling and before long Orr was forced to quit working out. Each day, he'd show up at the rink and watch the rest of the Bruins go through their preseason regimen. But while his teammates did their wind-sprints and the other routines hockey players use to get themselves in shape, Bobby sat in the empty arena and watched.

"It just acted up," said Orr, "so I decided to take a week off." But that one week stretched into another and before Bobby knew it, the season was almost ready to start.

With less than one week left before the regular season opened, Orr got the green light to start skating again. There was much to be done and very little time in which to do it, but Bobby approached the task with the enthusiasm of a rookie. He pushed himself to the limits of his capability, rushing to catch up with the rest of the Bruins.

"He amazed me," said teammate Phil Esposito. "He looked like he'd been playing for 20 practices."

The late start meant that Orr would miss all of the Bruins' preseason games, but Bobby made up for it by his work in the intrasquad games. He was easily the most active player on the ice in those last few days before the season began. And when the Bruins played their first game on October 11 against Detroit, Bobby Orr was ready.

"Bobby didn't have much of a training camp," said general manager Milt Schmidt. "But he was ready for the start."

The Bruins were being careful with Orr but that was no reason for their opponents to do the same. The Red Wings set the tone. Early in the game, Orr was skating easily with the puck cradled on the blade of his stick. He had just crossed into the center zone and cut to the right side when he came into Gordie Howe's range. Howe, always admired for his talent, but never for his gentleness, slashed at Orr's knee with his stick. The leg buckled but did not fold up. And inside, Bobby glowed with joy.

"He whacked me good," said Orr, "but the knee held up. I can't forget that one."

Shortly afterward, he had another one to remember. Orr had grabbed the puck in his own end and led a three-man rush up ice. As he charged into Detroit's zone, he was a stride offside. The linesman blew his whistle and Orr relaxed. Just then, Pete Stemkowski shoved his stick between Bobby's legs and Orr crumpled to the ice on his bad knee. He was up just as quickly but Coach Sinden was furious at Stemkowski's move.

"It was a cheap shot," muttered Sinden, "by a cheap-shot artist."

What was more important to Orr was that his leg did not pain him. It seemed strong and he proved it by playing almost half the game and scoring the winning goal in Boston's 4-2 victory. Had he been angered by Howe and Stemkowski?

"Listen," he said, "we all indulge in a bit of sneaky play; the little things. Those guys have a job; they have to get me. But they're good guys. In fact, you don't find many bad apples in this game."

Time after time, Orr came up against teams determined to test his fragile knees. There were bouts with every tough guy in the league. And each time he was dumped to the ice, Bobby would get up, dig his blades in and skate away, his knee still intact. There was one game against New York in December that restored Bobby's full faith in the limb.

Tough-guy Reggie Fleming, one of Orr's earliest sparring partners, caught Bobby with his head down behind the Bruins' net. Fleming headed straight for Orr, on a collision course that didn't take long to complete. Fleming caught Orr clean and hard and sent Bobby careening into the boards with a textbook check. Orr folded up like an accordion. If ever his knee would go, it seemed, this would be the moment.

But Orr rolled over and bounced up. He dug his blades into the ice and took off, making a mental note that he had a little score to settle with Mr. Fleming. But more important than that at the moment was the knee. It was sound.

"I'm not going to go skating right after a guy," said Orr, "but eventually, I'll let him know I remember him."

Sometimes it takes hockey players a week, a month, or even a season to get even with an opponent. It only took Orr one period to square matters with Fleming. He located Reggie and whacked him solidly, returning the Ranger's calling card. Fleming was impressed with Orr's retaliation.

"He's learned to be mean," said Reggie, a connoisseur of tough hockey. "He's learned that he has to stand up for his rights in this league; I can't blame him for that."

In the game against the Rangers, Orr demonstrated that he had lost none of the elusiveness that marked his first two seasons in the NHL. Early in the third period, goaltender Gerry Cheevers blocked a shot by New York's Rod Gilbert and cleared the puck behind the net to Bobby.

Orr cradled the puck on his stick and waited patiently, watching as the Bruins got set to move up ice. Slowly, Bobby moved around the right side of Cheevers' net, glancing up as forechecker Jean Ratelle moved at him.

As Ratelle closed in, Orr shifted to his left, leaving the Ranger flailing at empty space where, a moment before, the Bruin star had been skating. Now Orr was on his way. He moved over to the center of the rink, carrying the puck like a forward. Vic Hadfield ran at him, but again Bobby shifted speeds and was past the Ranger left winger.

Over the red line, Orr picked up momentum. There was no problem staying onside with Bobby. He was leading the attack now, not trailing it. Orr and the puck burst over the Ranger blue line and closed in on goaltender Ed Giacomin.

Defensemen Arnie Brown and Brad Park began converging on him, forming a pincer that would stop Orr but leave at least two

Boston forwards free. As daylight began to disappear with the two Ranger defensemen bearing down on him, Orr shoveled the puck to his left, where Phil Esposito was skating perhaps a stride behind him. With a snap of his quick wrists, Espo fired the puck.

Giacomin, preoccupied by Orr's rink-length dash, reacted a moment too late. He shot out his leg but the puck was by him and into the net.

The announcement was to become monotonous before the year was through. "Boston goal scored by Number 7, Phil Esposito," said the public-address man, "assisted by Number 4, Bobby Orr."

Playing flawless hockey, Orr led the Bruins to the top of the National Hockey League's East Division. His playmaking was sensational and he was setting up goals all over the place. And, even though he had to be concerned with defense, Bobby was doing his share of scoring too. Around the league, other players marveled at his play.

"He ought to get his name on the Vezina Trophy," said Esposito, the tall, happy-go-lucky center. "He blocks more shots than the goalies."

"He does so many things at once," said Billy Hicke of the Oakland Seals, "I think he's a committee of about nine guys."

Bobby and Toronto's Pat Quinn demonstrate that fighting goes hand in hand with hockey.

"That Orr," said the Rangers' Gilbert, shaking his head. "He seems to skate faster now than he did before. And he's got some new moves too."

"Just when you think you've got him lined up," said Jimmy Neilson, a tough-checking New York defenseman, "he gives you that little fake and . . . whoosh . . . he's past you again."

Orr was doing only what comes naturally. He was playing his game, convinced that his knees were sound and would hold up.

"I don't think about the knee when I'm out there on the ice," said Bobby. "It swells up after every game, but the swelling always goes away. The doctor said that would last about six months."

Orr not only was playing excellent hockey both on defense as well as up front, but he was also logging an enormous amount of ice time. Ninety seconds on the ice at a time is a normal player's usual limit. Few players log more than a total of 20 minutes on the ice in any single game but Bobby was closer to 40 night after night.

"I know I use him a lot," said Coach Sinden. "But I can't help it. Every time we're in trouble and I see him sitting on the bench, I throw him out there. I'd be crazy not to."

Few could argue with that reasoning. Bobby was the battery that kept Boston's energy flowing. And he was establishing a new style of play for defensemen. His rink-length rushes made him almost as dangerous offensively as some of the high-scoring forwards around the league. Never before had a defenseman rushed as often or as successfully as Orr. And because he carried the puck so often, he was a target, often being fouled two and three times in a single rush down the ice. He stood up for his rights but seldom lost his cool on the ice.

"I am surprised at Bobby," said Milt Schmidt. "Surprised that he has controlled his temper despite great provocation. Every time he goes out on the ice, he has the same problem as Gordie Howe or Bobby Hull. Players like these have the puck 70 per cent of the time and everybody is taking a run at them. I'm delighted to see Orr standing up for his rights. But you won't see him giving away any silly penalties."

Thanksgiving came and Bobby Orr had plenty to be thankful for. His team was in first place and his knee was holding up under the strain of three or four games and 40 minutes per game every week. Two weeks later, he had even more to be thankful for.

The date was December 16, 1968, and the Bruins were at home against the Chicago Black Hawks. Boston was trailing by a goal early in the first period when a Hawk was penalized. Coach Sinden sent Orr over the boards for the power play.

As play moved into the Chicago zone, Orr trailed the attack. Ed Westfall dropped the puck for him and Bobby cut for the net, shifting past the two penalty killers who were set to sandwich him. His powerful wrists snapped off the shot and it whizzed past the goalie, who seemed hypnotized by his move.

Now the score was tied, but not for long. A few minutes later, Orr corralled the puck behind his own net and started off. Past one checker and then another, Orr pushed the puck and headed resolutely toward the Chicago net. Playing like a man with a mission, Orr moved in and, once in range, he fired. Again, the puck flashed into the cords and the red light went on. Goal number two.

But Orr's basic job was defense and with the Bruins a man short, he later found himself on the ice killing a penalty, buying time with some fancy stickhandling, and waiting for his teammate, defenseman Don Awrey, to return from the penalty box. Just as Awrey stepped back on the ice, Orr located an opening. He swooped into the gap like an eagle. Forty feet from the net, Orr wound up and fired. The puck flew off the blade like a rocket leaving Cape Kennedy. No chance for the goalie; goal number three for Bobby Orr!

Three goals in a single game is hockey's hat trick. It's quite a feat for a forward but all but unheard of for a defenseman. But Bobby Orr isn't an ordinary defenseman.

Boston Garden exploded in cheers for the wonderboy who was turning the Bruins around. He was making this once rag-tag team into a contender with a new style of defensive play. The best defense, it has been said, is a good offense. Orr was proving that.

December became January and the Bruins stayed in front in the East Division. Orr played in the All-Star Game at Montreal and again was one of the outstanding performers.

As January started running out, the Bruins moved west for a road trip against Los Angeles and Oakland. On January 30 they were playing in the fabulous Los Angeles Forum which Jack Kent Cooke built to bring hockey to California.

Midway through the game, Orr was skating back to defend against a Los Angeles attack when his knee gave out and down he went. Sinden's heart skipped a beat as Orr limped off the ice.

"It might have happened to anyone," said Orr. "I was skating backward and my skate got caught in a crack in the ice."

Orr finished the game but his knee was sore — more sore than he was used to. "Naturally," he said, "I was worried."

The Bruins bundled Orr off to Toronto for an examination by Dr. John Palmer, who had performed the knee operation seven months before. Orr walked into the doctor's office with a frown and emerged with a smile. "I'm not worried now," said Bobby. "Dr. Palmer tells me I should be playing within three weeks."

The doctor's examination revealed that

Orr had irritated the lining of the knee but had not damaged the ligaments. A couple of weeks of rest would restore the limb.

With Orr and a couple of other Bruins sidelined, the first-place bulge disappeared. Montreal surged past Boston to cop the title and the Bruins had to be satisfied with second place. That meant a first-round playoff date with Toronto while the Canadiens were playing the New York Rangers in the opening Stanley Cup round.

The Bruins wiped out the Maple Leafs in four games and the Canadiens did the same to the Rangers. That set up a Boston-Montreal pairing for the semifinal round of the play-offs. It was a memorable series with the Canadiens winning the first two games on their home ice, then dropping the next two in Boston to square the series. In the fourth game, Orr jammed a short shot under Montreal goalie Rogatien Vachon for his first play-off goal.

The Canadiens took Game Five in Montreal and then Boston battled back in the sixth game, forcing it into double overtime. Finally, the agony of sudden death ended quickly and cleanly. Montreal's Claude Provost intercepted a clearing pass and found the incomparable Jean Beliveau cruising in front of the net. Provost's pass was on target and Beliveau's shot was low and true for the series-winning goal.

The Bruins' season ended that swiftly. For Orr, it had been a smashing success. He finished with 21 goals — an all-time record for defensemen — and 43 assists for 64 points, another record. He had broken the defenseman's record for goals by one over the mark established by Detroit's Flash Hollett in 1944-45. His 64 points were five more than the record for defensemen established by Chicago's Pierre Pilote in 1964-65.

Orr's performance earned him another All-Star berth and his second straight Norris Trophy as the league's outstanding defenseman. There was a difference about winning the Norris this time though. This time, when they gave it to him, he figured he had earned it. And when he accepted it, he wasn't on crutches.

And as the fury of another hockey season settled into the serenity of an Ontario summer, Orr kept remembering something Phil Esposito had said to him.

"We finished third my first year here," Esposito had said, "and second in my second year. That means next year, we'll win it all."

Orr could hardly wait for next year.

DICK RAPHAEL

Bobby Orr would accept the challenge of leading the Boston Bruins.

Chapter 11

BABE RUTH
ON ICE

THERE was a ghoulish slow motion to the way Ted Green fell to the ice, his eyes staring blankly into empty space after Wayne Maki's stick had come crashing into his head.

Green landed on his side and perhaps the scariest part was the expression on his face. It was not one of pain but rather one of confusion as if his brain could not comprehend what had just taken place.

The Bruins, who by now were being tagged the Gashouse Gang of hockey because of their carefree, rock 'em, sock 'em approach to the game, were in Ottawa for a preseason exhibition game against the St. Louis Blues.

Each NHL team plays a schedule of about 10 such games to give the players a chance to get into shape under game conditions. The unwritten rule among the athletes is to play an honest 60 minutes of hockey but not to take any chances that could result in injuries. Many players have not yet signed contracts and believe that an injury would damage their bargaining position with the clubs. Green expressed his feelings on that to teammate Derek Sanderson the day of that fateful game against St. Louis.

"I shouldn't even be playing tonight," Green told Sanderson. "I'm not going to hit tonight against St. Louis. I'm not going to get into any trouble. I don't want anything to do with this game — this exhibition — until I'm signed. When I'm signed, I'll start hitting. Then I'll play my usual game but until then, forget it."

But hockey is a contact sport and in the second period, the Bruins' Green found himself in contact with the Blues' Maki. There was the usual exchange of bumps between an attacking forward and a checking defenseman and play started moving back up ice, away from the Boston net where Maki and Green were still going at each other. Suddenly, there was the flash of sticks raised in the air — sticks, the one thing Bobby Orr feared most in hockey — and when it was over, Green lay crumpled on the ice, staring blankly into space.

Orr was on the Boston bench when Maki pole-axed Green. In a flash, Bobby was over the boards and on top of the rookie forward, belting him to the ice. Then he turned to see if he could help his fallen teammate.

Green was motionless, stretched out on the ice. He was trying to move but having trouble. When they carried him into the Boston dressing room, he said, "I'll kill that little bum." But the words were ominously slurred. There was obviously something seriously wrong with the defensive leader of the Bruins.

An ambulance took Green to a local hospital and it didn't take long for the doctors to find that Green's skull had been fractured. Maki's stick had cracked into the right side of Green's head, splintering some bone and damaging his brain. His left side was paralyzed and there was a dangerous blood clot. Immediately surgery was ordered, not to save Green's career, but his life.

The tragic episode cast a pall over the happy-go-lucky Bruins. It was as if time had stopped for the club when Green went tumbling to the ice.

"We couldn't be ourselves," said Bobby

Orr. "We could still see Teddy lying there."

The Boston management reacted by ordering all of the Bruins' farmhands to begin wearing helmets and then tried to get the varsity to do the same thing. But rather than impose the head protectors on the entire team, management ordered only defensemen to wear them.

The theory was that helmets would prevent any repetition of the Green tragedy. But there are built-in discomforts to them, such as perspiration, and it is almost impossible to ask an athlete who has been playing without a helmet for all of his life to suddenly put one on.

"I can't play with this thing," Bobby Orr told the Bruins. Milt Schmidt, the general manager, was at a practice when Orr shed his helmet. "Get off the ice," Schmidt bellowed at the defenseman. "Fine," Bobby replied, skating off and going to the dressing room. A moment later, rookie defenseman Rick Smith put his helmet down. Then veterans Dallas Smith and Don Awrey did the same. That was the end of the helmet idea and the beginning of Bobby Orr's move to a position of leadership with the Bruins.

The loss of Green left the Bruins floundering like a rowboat without paddles. A veteran of the dark days of the 1960's, Green had been the undisputed leader of the club. He set the tone with his rough-house play and, whenever there was a brawl on the ice, he was always the first man on the scene to help a teammate who might be overmatched. Now, with Green sidelined, the team's spirit sagged.

"With Greenie gone, there was no question about who had to be our leader," said Derek Sanderson, "but Bobby wasn't too crazy about the idea. He's a great kid, but a modest kid. One night after a game in Chicago, I sat next to him in the bus to the airport and told him he had no choice. We needed him, and he was it, whether he liked it or not."

Orr accepted the challenge. He pushed the rest of the Bruins the way Green would have had he been with the club. But he pushed none of them harder than he did himself. He took the burden of the defense on his shoulders and added to it the burden of the offense as well. Time after time, he would rush the length of the ice, trying almost singlehandedly to lift the Bruins. The challenge seemed to make Orr play better than ever. He was piling up goals and assists at an unbelievable pace and soared into the league lead in scoring as the season moved past its first month.

His scoring sent NHL statisticians scur-

Bobby shoots — and scores — against Montreal.

rying through the record books. Never in history had a defenseman led the league's scorers after the first week of the season. But here with the first month over, Orr was the leading scorer. How long could it last?

The perfect authority on scoring seemed to be Phil Esposito, Orr's talented teammate who had scored a record 126 points the year before. A newsman asked Esposito if he thought a defenseman could ever win a scoring championship.

Esposito thought for a moment and then answered, "Yes, if his name's Orr. When I racked up 126 points, I thought it would take a Stan Mikita or a Bobby Hull to come close to that mark. Now I have to put Orr right up there ahead of them. He's just too much.

"When I came to Boston three seasons ago," Esposito continued, "I thought Orr was an amazing skater. Last year, I thought he was amazing and fantastic. This season, he is amazing, fantastic . . . and I can't believe it."

In mid-season, with Orr obviously on the way to one of the most memorable seasons any defenseman ever had, another defenseman turned up in Boston for a press conference. Afterward, Ted Green walked down to the Boston dressing room.

"We were getting ready to practice," said Orr. "Teddy walked into the room and sat down right over there where he used to dress. His head was shaved from the operation and everything, and he didn't say a word. He just sat down, undressed, and started to put on his long underwear — as if he were getting ready for practice. As the guys came in, he'd look up and swear at them or give them a shot — just like the old Greenie, like nothing had happened. We were all right after that."

Green's visit gave the Bruins and Orr an emotional charge. The club needed it too. Locked in a five-team battle with Montreal, Detroit, Chicago, and New York, the Bruins needed every point they could get. Orr knew it and tried to lift the team before every game.

Bobby established a ritual before every period. He would sit in front of his locker with two hockey sticks, one in each hand, repeatedly lifting the sticks and letting them fall. Occasionally he would flick the stick with his powerful wrists, sending an imaginary puck into a nonexistent net.

Then, just before it was time to take the ice, Orr would stroll over to the locker Green had occupied when he was playing. Starting with the man occupying Green's space, Orr would move around the room, tapping the pads of every Bruin with his sticks.

"Bobby is the leader now," said goalie Gerry Cheevers. "You watch him with the sticks and, well, let's just say it could be pretty embarrassing for the guy who wasn't ready to play."

One night, one of the Bruins wasn't ready. When Orr approached, his teammate said, "Don't count on me for anything tonight. I feel lousy." Orr just grinned and then started betting the other Bruins that their ailing mate would score at least one goal that night. Sure enough, he got two.

The Gashouse-Gang spirit had been restored by the league's leading scorer, a defenseman named Orr. The way Bobby was scoring, his father, Doug, must have wondered if he hadn't made a mistake letting Bucko MacDonald, Bobby's pee wee coach in Parry Sound, make his son a defenseman. But the fact is that Orr was playing perhaps the soundest defense on the Boston club while doing all his scoring.

Midway through January, Orr scored his 65th point of the season, breaking the record for defensemen which he had established the year before. He already had 52 assists, breaking another record in half a season.

Orr hits the post, but the puck is in the Toronto net.

Yet he tried to play down his scoring heroics and chances for the scoring title.

"We're only a little more than half way through the season," said Orr, "and a few guys haven't started scoring the way they can. I never think of records or what I'm doing on the ice. Heck, I just do what comes naturally. In most cases, I suppose it's just a reflex action."

Despite his repeated rushes down ice, Orr was rarely caught out of position. That's because he was careful about when he took off.

"I look for the openings," said Orr. "If an opening develops, I go. If the opening isn't there, I stay back. I'm not trying to score goals for the record book. I just want to help the Bruins keep winning."

And as Orr kept scoring, the Bruins kept winning. The points kept rolling up for Boston in the standings and Orr in the scoring race. Finally, on March 15, Orr passed the 100-point plateau, scoring two goals and two assists against the Detroit Red Wings in a game that ended tied at 5-5. And his 100th point was typically Orr — a symbol of the kind of season Bobby was having.

Rick Smith was in the penalty box at the start of the second period when Orr located a hole in Detroit's power play attack. He lunged for it and Derek Sanderson saw him break. Sanderson fed him the puck and Bobby swooped down the ice, sidestepped Frank Mahovlich, and slipped the puck past goalie Roy Edwards.

"What can I say?" asked coach Harry Sinden. "I'm running out of adjectives. He was . . . well, he was just Bobby Orr."

Then Sinden reflected on Orr's season-long performance.

"I don't think everybody fully grasps what is going on," the coach said. "I'm convinced this kid is having the greatest season ever turned in by a professional athlete. Orr is more than a defenseman. You have to take the greatest efforts by individuals in any sport and match them against what Orr has done. This kid is hockey's Babe Ruth."

"Bobby is the most unorthodox defenseman I've ever seen," said Tom Johnson, a great defender in Montreal and now a member of the Boston front office. "You have to have great anticipation to do what Orr does. Bobby usually winds up with the puck and he had the best defensive record in the league."

What Orr does is to play the puck, not the man. Before Bobby, defenders would play the puck only in two-on-one situations. At other times, it was a man-to-man confrontation. But Orr prefers to skate with the puck carrier and take the rubber away without the traditional defender's tactics of the booming check. Orr plays defense like an artist painting a fine portrait.

As the season churned into its final week end, the NHL had the tightest race in its history. Five teams were battling for four play-off berths with Boston and Chicago tied for first place and Detroit, New York, and Montreal fighting it out for third and fourth.

On Saturday night in Toronto, the Bruins maintained the pace, whipping the Maple Leafs 4-2. The game's first goal, an unassisted one with the game less than three minutes old, belonged to Bobby Orr. It was his 33rd of the season. Less than seven minutes later, Orr fed Derek Sanderson for another score.

But Chicago beat Montreal so the Black Hawks and the Bruins were still tied going into the season's final night. Chicago had the edge in victories and unless the Bruins could finish with more points, they would end up second to Chicago.

Boston did its part, completing a week-end sweep of the Maple Leafs with a 3-1 victory in Boston Garden. Orr assisted on a tie-breaking goal by Johnny McKenzie for his 120th point, becoming the first defenseman in history to win the scoring championship.

Now the Bruins hurried to their dressing room to listen to the final period of Chicago's game against Montreal. The news was all bad. The Black Hawks had scored early and forced Montreal to open up what should have been a tight, defensive game. Once the Canadiens started taking chances, the game was lost. Chicago maintained the tie in total points but by winning five more games than the Bruins, the Hawks claimed first place.

Some of the Bruins were downcast over having to settle for second place, but once again Bobby Orr pulled them together.

"We have only ourselves to blame," said Orr. "I can remember half a dozen spots where we either settled for a tie or blew a game we should have won. We're the best team. The guys know it, and I know it."

And now Orr and his friends would get a chance to prove they were best in the play-offs.

Chapter 12

THE CUP

THE puck moved easily along the blade of Bobby Orr's stick, almost as if it was drawn by a magnet. Orr was in his own end of the ice, circling easily behind the Bruins' net. And he was playing his own personal game of shinny — stickhandling the puck, content simply to keep control of it, and in no great hurry to start an attack.

It was the opening game of the 1970 play-offs in Boston Garden and the Bruins were leading New York 3-1 early in the second period. When a Boston player was ordered to the penalty box, Orr was sent out to kill some of the shorthanded time. Coach Harry Sinden couldn't have made a better choice.

Orr is the perfect penalty killer because he has such good puck control. The long days and nights of stickhandling on the ponds of Parry Sound had made Bobby an expert at shinny — skating aimlessly around with the puck, concerned only with not surrendering the slippery rubber. And shinny is the best technique a penalty killer can use.

Earlier in the period, Orr had converted a perfect pass from Johnny McKenzie, firing a low, hard shot, that never got more than a couple of inches off the ice. The puck whipped past goalie Ed Giacomin for Boston's third goal of the game.

Now, with a Bruin in the penalty box, it would be New York's turn to press the advantage. And Orr was sent out to see that the Rangers didn't press it too much. Bobby was moving contentedly with the puck, killing the time the way a good penalty killer should, when he saw the hole.

He moved for it swiftly, suddenly turning on a burst of speed that made heads spin. In an instant, Orr was over the red line and bearing down on the New York net. He faked once, and then again. Now, with Giacomin down and at his mercy, Bobby flicked the puck into the net.

The old building on Causeway Street vibrated with the roar of the Bruins' fans.

Orr's second goal of the night — and a short-handed one at that — had put Boston in control. The Rangers, stunned by Orr's rink-length dash, played as if in a coma. Forty-four seconds later, incredibly, with New York still enjoying a manpower advantage, Derek Sanderson scored for the Bruins and the rout was really on. The final score was 8-2 and it could have been more than that.

"Don't be fooled by that score," said Orr in the dressing room. "This isn't going to be any easy series."

Bobby, as usual, was right, although the Bruins won the second game, this time by the score of 5-3. Orr's only point in the game was a third-period assist on a goal by Eddie Westfall, Boston's last score of the game.

The series switched to New York for Games Three and Four. When the Bruins skated onto the Madison Square Garden ice for their pregame workout, they were greeted by a gallery of angry signs and a chorus of catcalls. The Ranger fans were hungry for blood and they wanted the Boston variety.

New York responded with two tough-checking games, earning a 4-3 victory in the third game and a 4-2 decision in the fourth to square the series at two games apiece. The Rangers contained the Bruins, but they couldn't stop Bobby Orr. The splendid defenseman helped the Bruins slice a three-goal New York lead down to one in the final period of the third game, scoring his third goal of the series. Only a circus save by Giacomin in the final minutes deprived Orr of the game-tying goal.

Bobby also scored in the fourth game, cutting a two-goal Ranger edge in half with a third-period goal. Again, New York hung on to win.

That forced a pivotal fifth game in Boston. The team that won this one would be in the driver's seat, needing only one more victory to clinch the series. The losers of Game Five would be faced with the difficult task of winning two straight games.

The Bruins' dressing room was surprisingly quiet before the fifth game. The team knew what it had to do. They had the Rangers in a corner after taking the first two games and then let New York off the hook by dropping the next two. Now was the time to take charge. And it didn't take Bobby Orr long to do just that.

Less than three minutes after the opening face-off, Orr started one of his patented end-to-end rushes. He shed Ranger checkers one by one. Each New York defender had as much success stopping Bobby as a mosquito opposing a moose. With a style and grace that is exclusively his, Orr swept into the Ranger zone and boomed his fifth goal of the series past Ed Giacomin. Boston was on the scoreboard, put there by Number 4, Bobby Orr.

But the Rangers weren't ready to give up yet. They bounced off the deck, tied the score, and then took the lead. Late in the second period, Phil Esposito sliced Jean Ratelle's scalp by accident but picked up a five-minute penalty for drawing blood.

The worst part of Esposito's penalty was that he had to spend the full five minutes off the ice, no matter how often the Rangers capitalized on that manpower edge. Because he had drawn blood, the Bruins were forced to play a man short for the full five minutes. Earlier in the season, a similar penalty to Johnny Bucyk resulted in three New York goals and turned a close game into a New York rout. This was clearly the turning point of the series and Boston faced the challenge of the five-minute power play with its best penalty killers. Up front, it was Derek Sanderson and Ed Westfall who have made an art of killing time. And on defense, Coach Sinden sent out Don Awry and his partner, Bobby Orr.

The Bruins controlled the puck as if it

Time after time, Orr and his playmates broke
up Ranger attacks.

were a yo-yo on the end of a string. Time after time, Orr and his playmates broke up Ranger attacks. They rode out Esposito's five-minute sentence without allowing one really dangerous shot at their goalie, Gerry Cheevers.

Early in the third period, Esposito emerged from the penalty box and not long after that the rangy center whipped the tying goal past Giacomin. Now with the score at 2-2, the checking took over with neither team willing to take any chances at this point. It was obvious that breaks would make the difference. And the Bruins had the best break. After all, Bobby Orr belonged to them.

Sure enough, Orr turned the tide. He caught New York on a line change and quickly pressed the advantage, hitting Esposito with a pinpoint pass. Just as quickly, the puck was in the net and the Bruins were in front for keeps.

As the monotoned public address man announced the goal, bedlam broke loose in Boston Garden. The Bruins were in charge now, put there by Esposito and Orr, a combination that was becoming as famous in Boston as the Cabots and Lodges.

All that was left was the finishing touch on the Rangers and Orr took care of that himself, scoring two goals in the sixth-game

4-1 victory, including Boston's first of the game, and tying it with less than three minutes gone in the second period.

The two goals gave Bobby seven for the six-game series, a play-off record for a defenseman. There was a time when a defenseman who scored seven goals in an entire season was considered to be going pretty well. But Bobby Orr had scored that many in a week.

In the postmortems, Ranger coach Emile Francis kept coming back to Orr.

"He was the difference," said Francis. "He's the first one up the ice and the first one back."

Francis loves statistics and he was ready to prove just why Boston had won and his Rangers had lost this thrilling play-off-series.

"Their forwards outscored us by one goal in the six games," Francis said. "We didn't lose it there. But their defensemen scored eight goals and ours had two. That's where the difference was."

Unstated but understood was the fact that seven of those eight goals scored by Boston defenders were scored by Bobby Orr.

While the Bruins were finishing off the Rangers, Chicago's fired-up Black Hawks eliminated Detroit in six games. That set up a Boston-Chicago play-off semifinal that had some grudge aspects about it. First, it matched the Esposito brothers — Boston's high-scoring Phil and his goaltender brother, Chicago's Tony. Then there was the matter of Chicago's being awarded first place over Boston even though the two teams had finished the pressure-packed season with the same number of points. The difference was that the Hawks accumulated their points with more victories and that edge was worth $1,250 per man — the margin between what first- and second-place finishes are worth. But the money didn't bug the Bruins as much as the prestige. Boston hadn't finished first since 1941 and the Bruins also believed that they had the better team too.

But, like the Ranger series, the Bruins approached the semifinal against Chicago warily.

"They've got a great team," said Bobby Orr. "They've got good goaltending and a lot of scorers. I watched the Detroit series — part of it — on TV and Stan Mikita is going better than I've seen him all year. And their big guy — Bobby Hull — is skating like heck. It'll be a tough series, but I think we've got the horses."

The Bruins went into Chicago for the first two games of the series determined to get a split and deprive the Black Hawks of

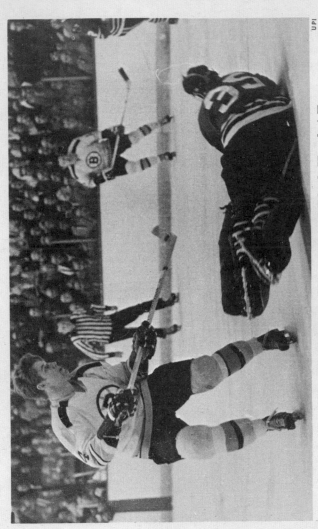

Bobby Orr scores against the Chicago Black Hawks' Tony Esposito in the play-offs.

the home-ice advantage their first-place finish had earned them. By finishing first — if by only a slim margin — the Hawks would have the home ice for their first two games, the fifth and the decisive seventh, if one was needed. That meant to win the series, the Hawks needed only to take each of their home games. Boston, on the other hand, would have to win a game on the road and the Bruins wanted to get that win in a hurry — preferably in the first game.

The Bruins were charged up for the series and their approach was reflected in something Phil Esposito said before the first game.

"If we lose," said the big center, "it will be because someone stops working and lets us down. Believe me, I'm going to be the first one on the guy who stops working."

But nobody — least of all Esposito — stopped working in the first game. Phil beat his goaltender brother Tony three times and the Bruins won 6-3.

"That's what we wanted," said Orr, "to win a game in their building."

The Bruins had come to Chicago intent on winning one game but they went home with two. With Orr totally dominating play, Boston won Game Two 4-1. The Black Hawks were standing around, seemingly hypnotized by Orr's super play. With five minutes gone in the second period, Bobby really dazzled them on one of his nonstop rink-long rushes. He eluded one, two, and finally three Chicago players.

Now at the Chicago blue line, Orr worked a perfect give-and-go with Fred Stanfield, shoveling the puck to his teammate and then taking the return pass without breaking stride. In a moment, he was on top of over-matched Tony Esposito and the puck was in the Chicago net for Bobby's eighth play-off goal.

Back in Boston, the Bruins went for the kill. "We're not going back to Chicago, boys," kidded Johnny McKenzie as the Bruins dressed for a practice session between the second and third games. "No way."

Just as he had been in the New York series, Bobby Orr was the man who was directing Boston's charge past Chicago.

"Bobby has learned how to control a game," said Harry Sinden. "Before, if we were ahead 4-1, he'd be out to make it 6-1. Now, he's learned to protect a lead."

Orr, averaging 35 minutes per game, was making it look easy. Midway through the third game, he charged behind the Chicago net, drawing three Black Hawk defenders with him, and then simply shoveled the puck in front to a host of unguarded Bruins just waiting to punch it past Tony Esposito.

The Bruins won that third game 5-2 as the Hawks battled furiously trying to find a way to beat Orr and the Bruins. Boston's tenacious checking was forcing Chicago to shoot on goalie Gerry Cheevers from long range or simply dump the puck into Boston's end and hope for the best. But with Orr on the ice, that tactic was simply useless.

"Whenever you do that," said Chicago coach Billy Reay, "you can just kiss the puck good-by. That's just another part of the game Orr has spoiled for everybody."

Mercifully, the Bruins finished the Black Hawks off in the fourth game, ending the agony in the shortest possible number of games. But Chicago didn't make it easy. Boston blew an early 2-0 lead when the Hawks connected three times in the second period.

The Bruins were down 4-3 in the third period but pulled themselves together with Ken Hodge tying the score and then Johnny McKenzie providing the clincher with less than two minutes left to play.

The quick finish to the Chicago series gave the Bruins a couple of days off while they awaited the outcome of the West Division semifinal series between Pittsburgh and St. Louis.

When the Blues eliminated the Penguins, Boston traveled to St. Louis for the first two games of the final series. Unlike the semifinal against Chicago, the Bruins weren't concerned that the home ice advantage belonged to the Blues because they had finished first in the West. After mowing down New York and Chicago, Boston was convinced there would be no trouble finishing off the Blues and claiming the treasured Stanley Cup for the first time in 29 years.

And the Bruins were right. Only once in the final round were they really in trouble and that was in the last game, when the Blues extended them to an extra period. But it only took 41 seconds of overtime for Bobby Orr's ninth play-off goal to seal the series and the Cup for the Bruins.

In the frantic dressing-room celebration that followed the final victory, Orr was ecstatic. Over and over he repeated the words: "Fantastic . . . fantastic . . . we've got a fantastic team. What a great bunch of guys, on the ice and off."

"I'm just glad," screamed Sinden in the middle of the frenzied scene, "that Orr scored the winning goal. It was only fitting after the year he had."

The Stanley Cup runneth over Bobby Orr.

The kind of year Bobby Orr had was 33 goals and 87 assists for 120 points during the regular season — 56 points more than any defenseman had ever scored before — and a record nine goals and 11 assists for 20 play-off points. The performance earned him his third straight Norris Trophy as the best defenseman in the NHL, the Hart Trophy as the league's Most Valuable Player, and the Art Ross Trophy as the scoring champion. When he also was presented with the Conn Smythe Trophy as Most Valuable Player in the Stanley Cup play-offs, it made him the first man in history to capture four trophies in a single season.

Chapter 13

A MAN FOR
ALL REASONS

A BOSTON grocer was about to ring up a sale when he took a second look at the $10 bill his patron had handed him. Oh, it was green all right and it felt like legal tender. But there was something that wasn't entirely right about the bill.

He looked at it a second time and there, smiling out at him from the spot usually occupied by Alexander Hamilton, was a portrait of Bobby Orr.

Down the street, campaigners supporting the election of Mrs. Louise Hicks, a Boston political figure, to Congress were handing out literature. Included was a Boston Bruins' schedule with the candidate's name liberally

UPI

Bobby "owned" Boston after the Bruins cap-
tured the Stanley Cup in 1970.

displayed on the front. On the back was a picture of Mrs. Hicks with Bobby Orr.

A local television station running a charity auction offered Bobby Orr's hockey stick autographed by his Bruin teammates. There were 152 bids on the item before it was sold for $1,000.

Indeed, Bobby Orr became the most popular player in the National Hockey League after leading the Bruins to the Stanley Cup in 1970. He received some 7,000 pieces of mail, which contained everything from proposals for marriage to pleas for help. Every letter was answered too. Orr would consider it impolite to do anything less.

"I get drawings, poems, letters, stuffed animals, and even love beads," said Orr. "I received letters from girls asking me to escort them to their proms."

Perhaps the most curious letter was the one from a man down on his luck who asked Orr for $10,000 to get started again. Bobby turned him down, but politely.

Bobby's attorney, Alan Eagleson, might not have been surprised if Bobby had written the man a check, though. Bobby does things like that sometimes.

"He's a bleeding heart and a do-gooder," said Eagleson. "And most of it's private. He doesn't even tell me about it. He doesn't

UPI

Bobby goes to a prom with Linda Geoffrion,
daughter of ex-Montreal star Bernie Geoffrion.

get receipts, and we lose all kinds of tax deductions because he doesn't make a record of it. Every once in awhile, he cleans out his whole wardrobe and gives it to the priest for charity. He'll get $500 for an appearance somewhere and he'll give it to the first charity worker he sees."

Orr became chairman of the Muscular Distrophy Association of Canada, the United Fund of Boston, and the March of Dimes, among other things.

"But that's not where his time goes," said Eagleson. "His time goes in visiting hospitals, orphan homes, poor kids, things like that. It's more than a duty with him. It's an obsession."

Orr doesn't like to talk about his charitable activities. He is almost embarrassed by them.

"O.K., I'm lucky, right?" he said. "I've been gifted, right? But the world is full of people who've not been gifted. Not only haven't been gifted, but have had things taken away from them. All I have to do is see one of them — some little girl that can't walk and yet she keeps smiling at me . . . all I have to see is someone like that and then I don't think I'm such a big hero any more. I think that compared to those people, I'm a very small article. A very small, lucky article. It knocks me down pretty fast. It cuts deep into me and I'd rather not talk about it."

Bobby off the ice is just an average 23-year-old. On the road, he frequently goes to the movies and enjoys walking around the cities the Bruins visit. "I enjoy people-watching and window-shopping," said Orr. He also watches a considerable amount of television.

When he's at home, Bobby can't stick his nose out of the door without being swamped by fans.

"When we lived in Lynnfield [a Boston suburb] the kids in the neighborhood found out we lived there. They came by every day to talk and get a piece of paper signed. At first I couldn't believe it. But it was fun talking to the kids. They're great."

Bobby spends most of his summer with youngsters at the hockey camp he operates with teammate Mike Walton. There's basketball, baseball, swimming, and other activities on the camp schedule besides hockey. And Orr delights in it all.

The summer after the Bruins won the Stanley Cup seemed to fly by for Orr. Before he turned around, it was time to start training camp again. Time for another 76-games of National Hockey League action. But these

Bobby Orr and teammate Derek Sanderson
have some fun at a practice session.

76 games would be like none ever played
before for Orr and the Bruins.

Again, Orr got off to a flying start, scoring and setting up goals game after game.
There was one difference though. This time,
he wasn't leading the league. This time,
teammate Phil Esposito was setting the
pace and two other Bruins, Johnny Bucyk
and Ken Hodge, were charging right along.
For weeks the quartet of Bruins occupied
the top four spots in the NHL scoring race
and two other Boston players, John McKen-

zie and Wayne Cashman, were running a shade behind them. Only Chicago's Bobby Hull was spoiling a Boston sweep of the top six slots. It was an unprecedented offensive show.

The scoring of his teammates had Orr all smiles. At last he wasn't getting all of the attention. At last people were realizing how good his teammates were too.

Over and over, Orr had emphasized that his 120-point season the year before wasn't only due to his own play.

"First, you have to realize the kind of team we had," Bobby said. "The Bruins were a team that controlled the puck for a lot of minutes in a lot of games last season. We also had many players who penetrated well. That meant that even though I was a defenseman, I was often in close enough to get off a good shot. The rest of it was just plain luck.

"I got some big goals, and I earned them. But I can't tell you how many times I shot and the puck went into the net off somebody's skate, or shoulder, or pads. It was the same with my assists. I'd get boxed in and have to shoot a blind pass, and it would land on a teammate's stick. He'd score a goal, and I'd get an assist I really didn't deserve. Everything went right for me — everything."

And 1970-71 was more of the same. Boston soared to the top of the East Division race and stayed there. Only New York posed any threat to the Bruins and the Rangers never really were in striking distance.

The Bruins rolled up 57 victories and 121 points — only two of 35 records they set in their sensational season. Esposito scored an unbelievable 76 goals and 76 assists for 152 points to win the scoring championship. Orr, incredibly, finished with the unprecedented total of 102 assists to go with his 37 goals. That gave him 139 points — 19 more than he had totaled the year before when he took the scoring title. But this time he finished second to Esposito.

Third and fourth places went to Bucyk, who had 51 goals and 116 points, and Hodge, who finished with 43 goals and 105 points. It was the first time in history that a single team had four players claim the first four spots in the scoring race and, of course, it was also the first time that four members of the same team scored 100 points or more.

The Bruins totaled 399 goals averaging five goals per game. The scoring fireworks at times bordered on the bizarre and Boston loved it. The town went wild over the Bruins and the passing of the Orr $10 bills was just one example of the daffy reaction of the rooters.

In March, Orr took time out to fly down to New York for the Muhammad Ali-Joe Frazier heavyweight championship fight. He had a front-row seat, rubbing elbows with the famous people who always turn up at such events. Actor Burt Lancaster, hired to do the fight broadcast, noticed Orr and sent word that he'd like to meet the young hockey star. Bobby was flabbergasted.

"Imagine," said the young man who had set the hockey world on its collective ear, "someone that famous wanting to meet me."

His shyness and humility have never deserted the young man, no matter how many goals or how many assists he has scored.

A few weeks later, the Bruins were ready to defend their Stanley Cup title. Their first-round opponents would be the Montreal Canadiens.

For hockey players, the Stanley Cup is the Holy Grail. A team can finish in first place — as the Chicago Black Hawks did in 1970 — but if they don't win the Cup, the season is a washout. When the 1970 season is remembered, it is remembered as the year the Bruins won the Cup, not the year the Black Hawks finished first.

"There's nothing as important to me," said Bobby Orr, as the play-offs began, "as keeping that Cup in Boston."

There was a rumor at the start of the play-offs that Orr was favoring a bad leg. His skating had seemed somewhat labored in the final weeks of the season and the new Boston coach, Tom Johnson, even sat him out, using Bobby only on power plays for four games after the Bruins clinched first place.

"My leg is fine," said Orr, a bit irritable over all the speculation. "And if it weren't I wouldn't be telling you anyway."

In the opening game, Boston's first goal was scored, predictably, by Bobby Orr. After the Canadiens tied the score, Orr assisted on Boston's tie-breaking tally as the Bruins won 3-1.

Game Two started off like another one-man show. Orr scored one goal and assisted on three others as the Bruins rushed to a 5-1 lead in the first two periods. Then, suddenly, like a balloon punctured by a pin, all of the air rushed right out of Boston. Montreal scored six goals in the third period to win 7-5.

The series moved to Montreal and now the momentum rested with the Canadiens. And they took advantage of it, shutting out Orr and beating Boston 3-2 in Game Three. Now the Bruins were in trouble. They needed a lift in a hurry and they got it from Bobby Orr.

Bobby scored three goals in the next game — the first time in 44 years of Stanley Cup history that a defenseman had scored three in a single game — as the Bruins won 5-2 to even the series at two games apiece.

In the pivotal fifth game, Orr assisted on three more goals and the Bruins romped to a 7-3 victory. One more victory and the dangerous Canadiens would be finished. But Bobby and the Bruins never got it. Montreal rebounded with an 8-3 victory in the sixth game and then won the series, beating Boston 4-2 in the seventh.

Orr had finished with five goals and seven assists in the seven games, a performance not unlike the one he had in the opening round against New York the year before. But the thing people remembered this time was Jacques Lemaire stealing a puck from Bobby in Boston's end at the start of the third period of the last game and feeding Frank Mahovlich for the goal that all but finished off the Bruins.

In the dressing room, Orr took the blame.

"Tom Johnson [the rookie coach] isn't to blame for this," Bobby began. "He made

all the right moves. There's nothing he did wrong and don't let anybody blame him. A lot of people will want to blame him but they can't. Tell them to blame me. I made the mistakes. Tom didn't."

A few weeks later, the Canadiens and Chicago Black Hawks had advanced to the Cup finals. Midway through the series, the NHL paused for its annual awards luncheon. On display were all of the handsome trophies the league hands out for achievements during the year. Standing in the middle of the hardware display was the Stanley Cup.

Bobby Orr, suntanned and dazzling in a blue pin-striped suit, stepped forth to accept his two awards — the Norris Trophy for the fourth consecutive year as the league's best defenseman and his second straight Hart Trophy as Most Valuable Player.

He stepped up to the microphone, cradling a trophy in each arm, and addressed the audience. After a few remarks, Orr turned to the corner of the room where the Black Hawk and Canadien players were sitting. Then he glanced back to the Stanley Cup.

"If any of you guys want to trade two trophies for one," said Orr, "I'm more than willing to make the deal."

The team trophy meant more to Bobby Orr than all of his individual awards.